D0874177

CONTENTS

PREFACE

The difficulty faced by many biographers is one of selection. How to make sense of trunk-loads of letters, how to keep a book within reasonable bounds. My problem has been the reverse. My mother was a private person, good at listening to others, hardly ever talking about herself. She kept no records of her earlier life, which is one reason why the first chapters are the shortest. Fortunately my father, Stephen Potter, comes to the rescue in two ways. Extracts from the unfinished and unpublished second volume of his autobiography are used in chapters three and four, covering his first meetings with my mother in the late 1920s and the early years of their marriage. Soon after the end of the period covered by this manuscript, Stephen started to keep extensive diaries, which I have only recently retrieved from the University of Texas. Chapters five, six and seven draw heavily on them. From about 1938, my own memory also begins to make a contribution; and for the later chapters I have interviewed surviving friends. If the final chapter is disproportionately long, that is partly because the period covered is better documented and more people are still alive to talk about it.

There is however some logic in the imbalance. If information about the early years is sparse, so unfortunately is the number of paintings that have survived. Each chapter describes the background to her work at the time and it is right to devote more text to Mary Potter's much more productive later years.

ACKNOWLEDGEMENTS

Many of those featured in this book have helped me with their memories and I would particularly like to thank Lady Meynell (Bay) and Mary Merrington (Mary Allen) in this respect, as well as so many others who have unstintingly given me their time.

Officials of the Harry Ransome Humanities Research Centre in the University of Texas have been assiduous and patient in sending me photostats of the relevant sections of my father's diaries. In the Red House chapter I have also made use of material from the diaries of Imogen Holst and I am grateful to Rosamund Strode for allowing me to see these.

Frances Spalding read the first draft of the text and I am grateful to her for her encouragement and helpful comments at the time and for her continuing support since then.

Most of the photographs of the paintings were taken by Douglas Atfield of Swilland, near Ipswich. Other photographers are named in the List of Plates. Public galleries and public collections have themselves supplied the photographs for the paintings that they own.

Financially, the book would not have been viable without generous help from the Britten-Pears Foundation.

Finally, I thank my wife Valerie, without whose persistent pressure and administrative help the book would never have been completed and whose comments on the text have been invaluable.

INTRODUCTION

by Julian Spalding, Director of Glasgow Museums and Art Galleries

Mary Potter's paintings strike one at once as being about reflections on light. It is difficult to define the quality of this light, for it is not of this world, nor out of it, but seems to occupy a special place of its own in between. It is certainly not the sparkling fresh light of the Impressionists, nor is it Post-Impressionist incandescence, though these artists were a major influence throughout her life. Nor is her light a moral battleground between good and evil as in, say, the vibrant chiaroscuro of Hogarth. Nor does it appear with a revelatory gleam, as in the sketches that Constable made of her chosen county, Suffolk. Mary Potter lived further to the north and east than Constable, at Aldeburgh, where dunes and pines, gorse and reeds edge up to the sea and where the light seems to be reflected back from everything, filling the clear air with a sensation of whiteness. But even this strange light does not fully account for the glowing quality of her pictures.

Latterly, Mary Potter seldom worked directly from life. The studio built for her later in her life had no views of the surrounding scenery. It was a white well, filled with a cool, bluish light that poured down from the high, north-facing window. Here she was detached from direct experience and could re-enact and work on the visual sensations that interested her most. These, in the main, sprang from her immediate environment: a breakwater in the sea, some flints on a sill, a fallen leaf on a path or light in a porcelain sink. But whatever the origin, and increasingly as her work matured, the specific sight recedes to a shade as the painting itself takes shape in her mind.

It is difficult to describe the creative process that changes a painting into a work of art. In Mary Potter's case it is particularly difficult because we have no words to describe the colours, shapes and textures that eventually coalesce on her canvases, obliterating everything else. Their very indeterminateness, one feels, is an essential quality sought by the artist. She appears to have (and this increased with age) a dislike of anything predictable; no shape, however simple, remains unbroken, no colour stays unscumbled, no light unshaded. This then is in part her painting process: she makes and then unmakes. And as her confidence in what she wanted grew, she developed the ability to do both at once: her apparently offhand flicks of the brush integrate and disintegrate in one action.

Eastern art and philosophy had a profound influence upon her, as they did on her close friend and neighbour, Benjamin Britten. *The Mere* (1958, fig. 1) has many similarities with Chinese painting but, despite the bending reeds, is no pastiche. It is the result of the discovery of a genuine affinity, though using a different medium (the Chinese did not use oil paint). Mary Potter's watercolours, which one might expect to be even more like Chinese painting than her oils, are usually quite the reverse in fact, revealing a tighter, though still sensitive, relationship to nature. They are studies before the contemplative experience begins to flower in the studio. As such, they reveal her other roots in the great English watercolour tradition which reached such heights with the Norwich School and was sustained into Potter's own student years by Wilson Steer.

Mary Potter's paintings could, however, never be described as romantic, despite their origins in the Romantic School and their closeness to the neo-romantic revival led by her contemporary, Graham Sutherland. Her work is not emotionally expressive; she does not throw herself passionately into a subject, but instinctively seeks a detached position. A sense of calm restraint gathers when a group of her works are shown together. It is not an easy sensation; the calm is convincing because the feelings restrained are strong.

Fig. 1 *The Mere* 1958 20 × 30 in.

This calmness owes much to sheer hard work. From the start she was determined to be an artist. Despite obstacles and with the help of a supporting role as a portrait painter, she succeeded, slowly and securely building up a small and highly enlightened clientèle who remained her supporters throughout her life. More importantly, the calmness in her art owes much to her philosophical and artistic outlook. To call her a Taoist would be misleading, and given her dislike of categorisation, offensive. But the Taoist detachment from, yet alertness to, life seems particularly apt when contemplating her art. Apart from a brief period in her youth, she did not teach. One feels she would have been sympathetic to the Tao story of the student who, having sought a particular teacher for many years, eventually comes across him sweeping leaves. The teacher refuses to speak to the student and he goes away. It is only a year later when the student finds himself sweeping leaves that he understands what the master has taught him.

Mary Potter takes a deceptively casual attitude to composition. She paints objects in a still life, or the view from a window, just as it happens to be, not with any special arrangement or juggling with the forms. They are casual gatherings, rather like the relatives at a family funeral who are invited not so much by ties of blood, but by the event. She seeks this casualness, of course, deliberately. For Potter the act that unifies her subjects is the act of painting.

Mary Potter's respect for paint as a medium, for its nature and for the natural effects of oil paint brushed on canvas, dominates her art. She never strains the paint to make it render appearances more accurately or pushes it to create a bravura effect. She paints as if keeping a distance from her hand, allowing the brush stroke to flex and break without any attempt to check or tidy its natural movement. The marks she makes only approximate to appearances. It is in this half language of signs and strokes that Potter found the freedom to develop her art.

Graffiti, child art and the paintings and writings of Paul Klee helped her in this direction. Her early work of the 1930s shares something of the *faux naïf* quality that was the mode then, following Ben Nicholson and Christopher Wood and the genuinely naive artist, Alfred Wallis. Their paintings demonstrated that the conventions of landscape painting, both academic and Impressionist, could be reinvigorated by adopting an innocent approach. Potter shows this innocence in her choice of unremarkable, almost banal motifs, like a child with its first camera, just aiming for the sheer fun of it. Even then, Potter realised that the informal image gave more scope for the development of her art.

The first step towards maturity involved abandoning the descriptive, sensitive brushwork of her post-student days. In its place she adopted a gawky, clumsy, child-like stroke that invigorated the picture with movement and, importantly for her later development, let the brush marks and the oil paint carry more of the message. She did not, however, allow this innocent charm to break the rules of perspective. Only in her very late work does the sense of gravity become displaced, but never, even then, entirely so. It was important to Mary

Potter that the sensations she created in her pictures remained physical. This desire explains both her use of thick impasto, worked with the brush or knife, and later her looser handling. A richly textured surface was a feature of Nicholson's and Wood's painting but it is to Wallis that one turns to discover how paint can be used to convey both light and the physicality of paint simultaneously.

In Mary Potter's paintings light does not annihilate substance. She rarely painted a direct light source, preferring it diffused or reflected back from a rough surface, or hovering, ghost-like, in shadow. She tended to mix white with her colours because she preferred them to be opaque and earthy. She avoided the otherworldly glamour of stained glass and never used a transparent coloured glaze. To modify a colour, she scumbled one over another, leaving both undisguised. This is painting, not appearance. Her colours, too, are offbeat, not natural. Greens abut with lilacs, salmon with grey. The tonal closeness of these hues allows the warmer tints to glow, the cool to recede. Though there is a touch of white in everything, we do not experience that consistent pale harmony which is such a feature of Paul Nash's art. In Potter's work the spatial play, the overlapping webs of colour, the surprising pure notes suddenly discovered, all create a sensation of vitality that is absorbing and astringent.

In one of Paul Nash's most famous paintings, *Pillar and Moon*, the white stone ball on the pillar rhymes with the lunar sphere. Both are painted in a similar way and exude a similar light, suggesting a continuity of luminosity between the terrestrial and the heavenly. Mary Potter's painting *Rising Moon* (plate 13) explores the same juxtaposition but the moon and the ball are worlds apart, in luminosity and texture. It is the light between them that interests Potter; the rising, misty blue that is neither real nor ethereal, the shadow thrown by the wall that glows with purples, oranges and greens hidden from the bleaching light. It was in this in-between light, between the spiritual and the physical, in the unreal world of art, that Mary Potter revealed a richer life. Throughout the 1960s and the 1970s, when the art world was painfully divided between abstraction and figuration, she confidently and imaginatively straddled both. Time will, I believe, reveal that her paintings were as 'modern' as any of her age. They will live because they glow in the mind.

CHAPTER 1

NEITHER
A BAPTIST...

M arian Anderson Attenborough – Mary to her family and to her later friends – was born on 9 April 1900. The three houses she lived in as a child were 'Rockford', 'Firbank' and 'Heathfields'. All in or near Beckenham, each one was more solid and respectable than the last. The size of 'Heathfields' reflected not only the increasing prosperity of the Attenboroughs, whose family firm of solicitors was doing well, but also the need for more room for the growing number of servants and for Jack and Mabel, my mother's younger brother and sister.

Both Arthur and Kathleen, my mother's parents, came from similar backgrounds. Their families were well-to-do and professional, mostly living in and around Bromley and Beckenham. They were closely linked by marriage: of Arthur's nine aunts and uncles on his mother's side, three had married Attenboroughs. It was an interdependent circle of friends and relations, held together by similar religious beliefs, professional interests and common codes of behaviour.

Arthur was a Baptist and religion played an important part in his household, beyond the conventional observances in those days. Prayers were held every day before breakfast, when family and servants gathered in the morning room and my grandfather presided. On Sundays, best clothes were worn and no games were permitted. Grandmother used to read the Bible from cover to cover, and when she had finished it she would start again. Her method was to read a chapter last thing – every single evening.

As Mary grew up, she seemed at first to fit well into the conventional pattern provided for her. A good eye, combined with a ferocious determination, led to early sporting successes at the local school, St Christopher's. She won prizes at swimming and diving; she represented the Southern Ladies at lacrosse. This determination, so conspicuous in later life with regard to her painting, was earlier applied to all her activities.

At St Christopher's, one of Mary's friends was Enid Blyton, the future author of bestselling children's books. In the holidays, Mary introduced Enid to Seckford Hall, then much dilapidated, now one of Suffolk's best-preserved Tudor manor houses. From time to time the Attenboroughs were invited to make use of part of this Hall for holidays. It was an hour by horse and trap from Ipswich station and these visits were Mary's first to East Suffolk, where she was to live for the last thirty years of her life.

At school Enid Blyton organised with Mary a group called 'Mauve Merriments'. The players dressed in mauve with white ruffles and black pom-poms: Attenborough took the leading parts, Blyton played the piano. Together with another friend, Mirabel Davis, Mary and Enid also started a new school magazine – *DAB*. Davis wrote the poems, Attenborough did the pictures and Blyton contributed the stories. No copies can now be traced, but it is probable that Mary's illustrations were similar to those of Willebeek Le Mair, an illustrator she much admired. Aged fourteen, she did a number of watercolours in his style, some of which survive as carefully treasured Christmas cards.

In fact Mary started to draw and to paint even earlier than this. As a young child, she would be found drawing in bed well after she was supposed to have been asleep. She seems always to have known that she wanted to paint and later tended to assume that any other serious artist would have had similar intimations. She had come to realise that although St Christopher's was a good school and she was doing well there, it could not offer her the specialist training she wanted. At the age of fifteen she was told that she would be head girl from the following May. But it was now decided that she would only do this for one term, would leave early and go to the Beckenham School of Art in the autumn. This meant leaving before she had matriculated, and was not in accordance with her parents' earlier expectations. They cannot have been happy with the new plan.

All that is known about Mary's two years at the Beckenham School of Art is that she was taught by Miss Amy K. Browning* and that she won first prize for portrait painting. She was then awarded an exhibition scholarship to the Royal College of Art, but she did not take this up. Instead she went to London, called unannounced on the Slade School, and asked to be enrolled. She not only got a place, but also an Orpen bursary on the strength of her RCA award. The Slade was her preferred choice and there she went, at the age of eighteen-and-a-half, starting in October – the month before the Armistice.

For three years Mary commuted from Beckenham, and the contrast between her student life in town and the restraint in the evenings must have been marked. Kathleen and Arthur were saddened by her non-observance of Baptist practices and perhaps by her obvious preference for Gower Street. If this led to any friction at home, it does not appear to have lasted. I never heard my mother refer to either of her parents other than in terms of love and affection; nor did I ever hear a word of disparagement about her Beckenham background.

* Wife of portrait painter Tommy Dugdale and a notable artist in her own right.

CHAPTER 2

...NOR A BOHEMIAN

At the Slade, students of both sexes were known by their surnames. 'Attenborough', however, was too cumbersome, and quickly got shortened to 'Att'. Until middle age my mother was generally known as Att, and surviving friends from those early days always called her by that name.

Att had been determined to get into the Slade and, once there, she was not disappointed. Like students anywhere, those at the Slade knew how to enjoy themselves and Att's social life blossomed. Many of the friendships she formed were to last for life. For some, the work may have taken second place, the School being regarded as a fashionable alternative to university, or as a social centre for London life in a break between war service and permanent jobs. But there were many who, like Att, were at the Slade to equip themselves to continue as full-time artists.

Att's main teacher was Henry Tonks, who had been assistant professor under Frederick Brown since the 1890s and who in 1919 succeeded him as professor. She drew according to his precepts. Students had to face the hard slog of drawing (it was a long time before they were allowed to paint), first from plaster casts of the human form and later from nude models (fig. 2). These, whatever their imperfections, were not to be beautified. Tonks's teaching was a conservative call to order, demanding that students should look hard at the object before them and depict exactly what they saw. In this the Slade was aligned with the New English Art Club, which had originated in 1896 as a French-inspired call to non-romanticised realism. Both the NEAC and the Slade had criticised the teaching at the Royal Academy for allowing students too much latitude in their interpretations. Since then however the 1910–1911 London exhibition of Post-Impressionists, which included paintings by Cézanne and van Gogh, had sparked off a schism in the NEAC and led to the formation of the London Group in 1913. In 1918, Tonks was still disregarding the impact of Post-Impressionism, even though many of his former pupils began to join the London Group.

However out of touch Tonks's teaching may have been with what was going on elsewhere, Att always maintained that she had benefited from it. But she did not accept everything he said without question. There was a particular issue between them: when she was permitted to progress from drawing to painting, she wanted to use a lighter range of colours than the dark tones prescribed by the professor. Frances Spalding wrote in a 1977 article in *Studio International* how once, '… after much castigation, she painted in a fury a sunburnt Amazon against terrestrial gloom and followed this with a walk on Hampstead Heath to cool her temper. On her return to the Slade she met Tonks in the Hall, and to her surprise he said of her joke effort: "much better".'

It shows intrepidity to have even thought of arguing with Tonks. One contemporary student has written: 'Even if you passed him the other side of Tottenham Court Road, you took your hands out of your pockets'. Whenever he entered the Life Room, the students would fall silent, wondering who would be the target of his sarcastic barbs. Fortunately the professor must have been sufficiently flexible to accept wayward methods of work by those he thought talented. Six years earlier, he had praised the work of Stanley Spencer, despite its eccentricities. Two years hence, he was to praise the work of Rex Whistler, who would only draw from memory, with fanciful embellishments, and not directly from the object in front of him. So now Att, in spite of her deficiencies, became one of Tonks's star pupils. The Orpen bursary had financed her for one term only, but now she was awarded a two-year scholarship. Eventually, Tonks even admitted that her pale tones had quality.

Off duty, Att had a wide array of friends. Mary Hope Allen, who was later to make a brilliant career in the Drama and Features department of the BBC, was one of the few prepared to stand up to Tonks – and, later, Lord Reith. While many of the students came from respectable suburban homes like Att's,

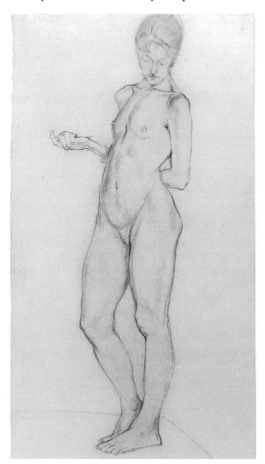

Fig. 2 Slade drawing 1920

16

some had more exotic backgrounds. Clare Mackail was Burne-Jones's granddaughter and used to take Att to her father's house, which was full of William Morris furniture and Pre-Raphaelite paintings. Reine Ormond, who was Sargent's niece, became a lifelong friend. Later, my father Stephen Potter described her in these terms: 'Reine, the muted voice, the perfectly poised, the understanding. Att admired her so much – and thought her a superior being'.

A contemporary who soon after leaving the Slade briefly held the reputation of being the most promising artist of her generation was Winifred Knights – known exclusively by her surname. She had in 1920 become the first woman ever to win the Rome scholarship in Decorative Painting (Prix de Rome). After the Slade, Knights lived in Italy and married Tom Monnington, also a Slade student and Prix de Rome winner.* Att was one of the first to be told of their engagement. While she kept up with Knights until her early death in 1947, she did not see a great deal of Monnington in later life, and when he became President of the Royal Academy in 1966, it seemed as if they were poles apart, since she had always held herself aloof from that institution. The gap between the Slade and the Academy gradually narrowed, but Att never entered paintings for its Summer Exhibitions and withstood all blandishments to do so. Yet in 1973 she finally dropped her guard, to the extent of accepting Monnington's invitation for her to be guest of honour at the Academy's annual dinner. They enjoyed reminiscing about old Slade friends, and she was to be invited again.

Another dedicated student was John (Jerry) Howard, who in his eighties affectionately remembered Att as his oldest friend. He was one of those lucky enough to have a studio nearby – in his case, a room in Charlotte Street previously rented by both Augustus John and Constable. At evening parties there it was usual to perform some 'turn' – a song, a skit, a dance – anything a bit different. Att knew a string of long narrative songs, some of them ribald. She accompanied herself on the ukulele while singing them, and they came to be expected of her.

Other more lavish parties were given by John Howard's friend Mike Harrison, who was not at the Slade but was a frequent guest of students and an open-handed host himself at his parents' sumptuous house (once Dante Gabriel Rossetti's) in Cheyne Walk. Here too Att would be induced to do one of her turns. As well as singing with the ukulele, she was also a good mimic, and like a proto-Ustinov, was able to imitate not just demeanour and accent, but also almost any conceivable noise, even the squeaking of a car door. One turn that I still remember myself was a take-off of the BBC's New Year's Eve programme. While my father did the over-earnest voices from all over the British Empire, wishing the King and his peoples a happy and prosperous new year, Att snorted out the inevitable atmospherics of those days, as she rubbed together a saucepan and frying pan for added effect.

---

* According to his sister-in-law, it was Monnington who first told Att about the technique of mixing Parris' Marble Medium with her paints. If so, then it was a tip of immense value, since from 1935 onwards Att always used the beeswax-based substance in this way. Moreover, as time went on she realised that it helped to preserve the colours: in 1963 she wrote a letter to Duncan Grant recommending its advantages.

From her Slade days onwards, Att always enjoyed parties; but while working, she was impervious to distractions. As she grew older, this single-minded determination was apparent to all who knew her: some were even alarmed by it. Then, it was obscured by her other talents and activities. But Jerry Howard saw what was happening. 'I admired her tremendous dedication to painting, which nothing could interfere with,' he said. 'It was the only thing she ever cared about.'

Wherever she lived, Att always seemed to find a new circle of close friends. On the one hand she was able to make people relax and laugh, on the other she had a calmness, a core of serenity, that made her a good listener and encouraged her friends to come up with their troubles and their thoughts. 'She was not a Bohemian,' said Mary Allen. 'Her attitude to life was generous and unfussy. Witty in a dry way, she was at ease and the most natural person I have ever met. She was wonderful in her placidity.'

Stephen Potter, Att's future husband, later wrote disparagingly of his own approach to writing when he was young 'when rule one seemed to have been never for a single instant to write with any consideration of the reader's desire to be interested or entertained'. At the Slade Att developed a professional attitude to her work which was also anti-commercial, but only in so far as it put her own standards before the opinions and preferences of the buying public. She always felt that she was a better judge of her own work than her patrons, and was loath to modify her work at their request.

Att left the Slade in 1921. She had won seven prizes, including the Slade scholarship in 1919 and first prize for the painting of a head in 1921. Tonks had for some time been taking her very seriously indeed, trying to stop her going to parties so that she could concentrate exclusively on her work. When she left, he wrote her a good reference and told her: 'You must never get married. You have got to give up *everything*.'

When six years later he heard that she had gone against his advice he exclaimed, with singular lack of prescience: 'It is a tragedy. Their work always deteriorates when they get married.'

Sources

Forge, Andrew, *The Slade, 1871–1960* (Three articles in *Motiv*).

Macdonald, Stuart, *The History and Philosophy of Art Education*, ULP.

Reynolds, Michael, *The Story of an Art School*, unpublished.

Spalding, Frances, *British Art since 1900*, Thames and Hudson.

CHAPTER 3

LIMBO

W hat happened to Att between leaving the Slade in 1921 and marriage in 1927 is difficult to unearth. She worked at painting – yet hardly any pictures from this time survive. This is strange, as she later claimed that family life interrupted her work as an artist and that for a number of years after marriage her output was low. This story has been taken up and embellished by successive authors of catalogue introductions. The implication is always that a rich outflow of paintings was suddenly halted. Yet only four or five of these have surfaced. So what happened to the rest? She may have re-used the canvases, painting over pictures she thought were not up to standard. She often did this later on, always being more interested in her current and future work than in what she had done earlier. Other paintings from this time may simply have got lost: she did not then have a regular gallery and there was no-one to catalogue and photograph her work or keep an eye on where it got to. For those still hanging on walls today, attribution would be difficult. She did not sign her paintings at this time and if there are any with a 'Mary Attenborough' label on the back, the present owners are unlikely to make the connection with Mary Potter.

Att's other activities are also difficult to trace. She rarely talked about this period and kept no letters. It is almost as if it was a time she had wanted to forget. Yet what scanty evidence there is shows that those years were in no way gloomy.

On leaving the Slade, Att did a brief spell of teaching at the Eastbourne School of Art, and for a year continued to be based in the family home. But this could not last. In the autumn she wrote to Knights: 'We're getting into our studio on Thursday – I'm working like hell all over the place – in Sargent's studio [Reine's uncle was in America], on the stairs here and in grandpa's billiard room!' 'Our' studio was to be her means of escape. Att and another Slade friend, Sine McKinnon ('Shiny'), were about to move into a rented room in Fitzroy Street, which runs into Charlotte Street, scene of so many Slade parties. They shared the costs, Att having been given a £3-a-week allowance from her parents. The plan was that both girls would paint there. In the event, Att lived there as well.

So ended the daily trek to her parents' home, which Att visited little in the next few years. She was able to spend more time on her work; but she allowed herself more diversions – many more than she was to permit herself in later life. She spent much of these years travelling around this country and the Continent. She stayed with Shiny's family in Argyll. She went on short holidays or expeditions with Reine Ormond or Clare Mackail, sometimes to Paris. With Ivy Mackusick, again from the Slade, she shared an antique wooden caravan, parked in a field near Hartfield, Sussex. She and Ivy also took paints and bicycles to Brittany and once the two of them went painting in Corsica, risking the bandits.

Clare Mackail was the link with another French connection – a farmhouse at Omonville, near Cherbourg. Clare had introduced Att to George and Margie Booth, whose relations the Warre Cornishes owned the farmhouse. The Booths had six children, the Warre Cornishes three. Every summer they massed at Omonville, together with a French family, the Geoffroy de Chaumes, who themselves had ten children. Surprisingly they also had room for non-family guests, and three or four times Att, who through Reine also knew the Geoffroys, was one of them. By the time she got to know Stephen Potter in 1926, her French was good and he was impressed by the way she used it to shepherd him through customs and chivvy up the porters.

Knights (soon to be Mrs Monnington) was visited by Ivy and Att at the British School in Rome in 1923 and wrote a letter to her mother about their stay. It is the only written evidence of Att's Continental travels in the early 1920s:

> I think Att and Mackusick enjoyed themselves very much. I took them all round and showed them the sights. We had a full week and went twice to the opera and once to the Marionette theatre, they both looked the picture of health and I saw them off to Arezzo, and then they were going on to Florence for a few days and then back to Cannes where Att is having a fine time at the Mackusicks' villa.

The detour to Arezzo was presumably to see the Piero della Francescas, and the visit must certainly have been encouraged by Knights and Tom Monnington. Both were under the spell of quattrocento artists: the influence of Piero della Francesca had been noted by critics in both their Rome prize paintings and Monnington had made a special study of Piero's work in Arezzo. Att too always revered him – an enthusiasm that may have begun with this first visit to Piero country.

According to Jerry Howard, such snippets do not reflect the extent to which Att was travelling about all over the place at this time. In later life, when the impression was one of stillness, painting the scene from the window of her home, Att used to say that when she was young she spent too much time going to parties and gadding about the Continent. Yet one of the songs she knew by heart was Schubert's *Father I long to roam*. She continued to sing this, accompanying herself on the piano, long after her constant travelling was over.

There was one other source of income to support these journeys. As Att's portrait prizes from the Beckenham School of Art and from the Slade suggest, she had the ability to catch the likeness of any sitter. Tonks did his best to look after his preferred students, and just as he later arranged for Rex Whistler to get the job of painting the walls of the restaurant in the Tate, almost as soon as he had left the Slade, so he arranged a number of portrait commissions for Mary Attenborough. The earliest portrait I can trace is of her grandfather, John Atten-borough, painted in 1923 (plate 1). The domineering face, eyes bleary with age, stands out from the Tonksian gloom of the rest of the picture. Possibly Att could have developed a career as a portrait painter, but she would not have been content to do so. She seems to have thought that the work was too easy and that her technique was getting too automatic – she decided not to accept any more commissions.

It is not clear whether Tonks continued to influence her other work. Despite his reluctant acceptance of Att's lighter tones, the only four Mary Attenboroughs I know of dating from this period are all much darker than her post-marriage work. *Evening Sketch* (plate 2) was painted when Att was still living at home, in about 1921; while *Girl with Ukulele* (plate 3), darker still, is dated 1922. Tonks's influence must have lingered.

When Att was not away, she worked in her Fitzroy Street studio. She exhibited regularly with the New English Art Club, and also with the Seven and Five Society. In 1921 (while still at the Slade), she had become an early member of the Seven and Five, exhibiting ten pictures in its 1922 show and four in 1923. The 1922 show won her, for the first time, praise from critics in the national press. *The Daily Mail* grouped her with a number of other exhibitors as showing remarkable gifts and adding to the attraction of 'this surprising show'. P. G. Konody of *The Observer* wrote:

> Not all the members of the group show the modern tendencies of the artists I have mentioned. Miss Attenborough proves herself a very competent and accomplished painter on more traditional lines. Her *Boy with a Flute* is a portrait study of remarkably rich quality, and *The Horse Show* a spirited, animated scene, almost a bird's eye view, painted with the looseness of touch needed to make this kind of subject convincing.

Att was never to align herself with groups or movements, so many of which were flourishing at this time. The Seven and Five began as a reaction against them and Att probably felt in sympathy with the Society's original manifesto, which said:

> The object of the 'SEVEN AND FIVE' is merely to express what they feel in terms that shall be intelligible, and not to demonstrate a theory nor to attack a tradition.

Many of the later members of the Seven and Five rank high in the list of the English artists that Att most admired: Henry Moore, Barbara Hepworth, Christopher Wood, David Jones, Ben Nicholson and Frances Hodgkins. To begin with, however, the society was, according to Seven and Five researcher Andrew Wilson, 'little more than a means whereby relatively little known or unknown artists could exhibit their work'. It made little impression on Att. In 1978 she wrote to Frances Spalding:

> The only three members were P. H. Jowett, whose work I didn't like much *then*, Claude
> Flight, whose work I can't remember, and Ivon Hitchens, who used to take me out to
> lunch! At that time he was doing grey, colourless affairs, all called studies of essential form!

Att resigned from the Seven and Five and did not join another group of any kind until 1930,
when she became a member of the London Group. She did this in order to have a vehicle for
exhibiting her pictures between her one-man shows, and not in order to identify her work
with a particular movement: the London Group in any case had become by then so diverse
that it could not be said to represent any particular style.

In the evenings, Att was not short of invitations. Her male friends were the antithesis of
her own iconoclastic character. Phil Nichols was a diplomat, already able to talk with inside
knowledge about global affairs. Alert and intelligent, he was able to charm and bring out the
best from people who appealed to him. They formed a close friendship that was to continue
for life and that later took Att to Rome, Prague and The Hague, the cities where Phil was
posted. Then there was the rich and sophisticated Mike Harrison. At some point in the
1920s, Att had been given a room in Reine's house at 94 Cheyne Walk. This was the street
where Mike lived. She saw a good deal of him at this time and according to Jerry Howard,
Harrison's best friend, 'if she had been going to marry anyone then, it would have been Mike'.

Gwen Herbert was an ex-Slade student of a slightly earlier vintage and she, Clare Mackail
and Att sometimes went sketching together. She and her husband Alan had a handsome
house in Hammersmith Terrace and it was at one of their boat-race parties that my mother
and father first met. Stephen, who taught at a crammer run by Gwen's mother, describes the
occasion in this extract from his unpublished book:

> I do happen to remember seeing a girl with large clear grey eyes who wore artist's
> corduroys. These clothes made me feel irretrievably undergraduatey. This girl was called
> by her surname, 'Attenborough'. Not a particularly attractive method of naming, I
> thought. It was a late afternoon boat-race … Wanting to talk about it I had to stand on
> the edge of a small group listening to Attenborough plonking on her ukulele and singing
> in a toneless, level voice a song about 'My Monday girl, she lives on Main and Broad'.
> All this was miles outside my scope … 'My Wednesday girl, she lives on cocaine beads'.
>
> I had never had contact with artists before in my life. Perhaps they could only paint
> with the help of some sort of artificial stimulus? Were they to be envied or pitied? The
> Attenborough girl seemed outwardly to have the skin and limbs of perfect physique.
> Rather typically of quite a lot of the women here, she didn't seem to go in for make-
> up. Her skin appeared to glow with unquenchable health. But appearances, I said to
> myself, can be deceptive.

A more prolonged meeting with Stephen came through the Omonville connection. He had
been invited there by another Booth/Warre Cornish relation. Att already knew the set-up

well. The Normandy farmhouse was filled with musical talent. Many of the ten Geoffroy and six Booth children later became professional or semi-professional musicians, so chamber music and singing was one evening occupation. Another was *Tableaux Vivants* – a version of charades well suited to Slade graduates, in which the actors imitated well-known paintings. Jerry Howard was another non-family guest at Omonville and he and Att mimed Landseer's *Dignity and Impudence* – he as the heavy-jowled bloodhound, she as the impudent puppy. They also did Manet's *Olympia*, she adopting the languid pose of the lady, he that of the cat.

Pitched into this crowd of Att's Slade contemporaries and younger fans, Stephen may at first have felt inhibited. Att was earmarked to escort him across the Channel, as he here describes:

As a start I was to be taken over on the *Carpathia* (first leg of her usual voyage to New York). I had been given an escort. This turned out to be the girl Attenborough, the painter. She turned up dressed in corduroy from head to foot, with a curious old hat. We explored the big liner. There was a fine expanse of deck which tempted Attenborough to run. She took little notice of me, seeming to enjoy running off by herself.

Omonville turned out to be a large low rambling house with a damp and undersized tennis court. The only person who could play tennis seriously was Attenborough, who was surprisingly good. I had thought of her as an 'artist' and therefore unlikely to share my daily itch for some game: but on the contrary. Her arm looked soft and delicate enough but her hands were firm work hands, and she gripped the racket fiercely. 'Like a tiger,' she used to repeat to herself – to my surprise. '*Tiger!*'

She and her Slade friend Ivy Mackusick painted watercolours. Ivy called Attenborough 'Att' or 'Attipops'. They both had this quickfire, abrupt way of talking. Sometimes it was difficult to hear. 'Jerry's-coming-over. He's-absolutely-priceless.' These two phrases were spoken as if they were two words.

Sitting on a wall, with her watercolour block on her knees she would screw up her forehead into a maze of lines. Officially neither Att nor Ivy could be talked to when they were painting. It was a drizzling-looking sky, the day and the landscape was as dull as lead. 'What *is* that, the shadow?' Att might ask me, meaning 'what colour?'. 'Just dingy dark?' 'There's a lot of purple in it', she corrected me. 'That's the funny thing. And specks of umber.'

I felt very easy with her. Most of these people came from comfortable houses. Att and I were from good old South London. We had the same sort of homes, the same sort of uncles and aunts. We had both broken away from 'the family'. London South was a link.

Besides the Booths and Warre Cornishes, various young men turned up, some a little older than me. They seemed to know Att. John Howard was an old Slade friend.

But Philip Nichols, all set for a brilliant career in the Foreign Office … there he was, as usual en route for somewhere exotic, spending 30 shivering hours on a Normandy beach. To see Att? Not entirely: but Att was not ignored.

She could stand cold water longer than me – I was out first and was able to approve, emerging from the sea, those fine firm thighs, the small feet, the brown shoulders and white breasts. I wished my eyes were as clear as the extraordinary Attenborough's – extraordinary because she allowed her hair to become a sort of tangled mass of seaweed.

Another good thing about Att was the fact that though perfect in body and with a wide cheek-boned attractiveness and a general aura of air, sea, beaches and sea-pebbles scrubbed by waves, she never seemed to think in terms of a possible love affair: so it was never implied that there should be spells of courtly admiration; nor was there the slightest atmosphere of tick-off if she had to light her own cigarette or carry her own suitcase – indeed she took any such attention as a mild bit of unexpected luck, by no means to be repeated.

One thing was certain: Attenborough was going to be my friend. As a start, when we got back to London I used to turn up twice a week in Battersea Park to play tennis singles, 12–1, on the good new public courts there. We might eat at a tea-shop, Dutch. We always went Dutch, except that I did take her to dance occasionally and did pay, though this may not have been such a treat as I thought, I realised, when I found that she had at times been accustomed to dance four nights a week … Soon after the opening of the Gargoyle I danced there with Attenborough, who wore a net and lace dress.

The enigmatic courtship, conventional wedding and far-from-perfect honeymoon that followed are all described in this further extract from Stephen's manuscript:

When was it exactly? Early April, it must have been. Who suggested the long weekend walking tour in the Newbury area? Ivy Mackusick? John Howard? Me? Attenborough?

Day One: fifteen miles. Then on Day Two, an event. I saw that Att felt that this rate of walking wasn't good enough. The grass was pale and chalky, the blades were jerked by the wind, the larks sounded very high and distant. Att thought a good run was indicated, or at any rate she couldn't hold herself back on a nice long downhill slope. She was wearing a yellow cardigan unbuttoned, and the wind made it fly out behind her. That dependable run. It was as if she had in mind some athletic star she admired as if it were manly, and this made it seem the opposite of manly. 'Doesn't she look marvellous, running like that' – I said to myself, but it was out loud and J.H. cast a scrutinising glance on me. He stared at me. Why did he stare at me? Had not something gone wrong? The very thing which most attracted me – the impossibility of falling in love with her – had not that gone wrong? Did I not in fact love Attenborough, most deeply? That evening, struggle as I might, I gradually lapsed into almost complete silence.

After about two days I wrote Attenborough a letter telling her that it would be painful for me to go on seeing her, that the best thing, if she didn't mind, would be for us to stop our casual meetings, which I had so much enjoyed. That for a little while, our two or three meetings a week must come to an end. Three months later, on July the 7th, at the Beckenham Baptist Church, we were married.

The auguries were not particularly good for Att and myself – there was not much to suggest that our temperaments fitted well and that we were set for many years of happiness, and the enjoyment of what was to be in many respects a classical 'perfect marriage'. To start with we had very little money. Money from her painting had scarcely yet begun: my income was £200 p.a. … Rather naturally, her parents thought that I should be encouraged to get down to it and support my wife properly, so they made it clear, before we were married, that they would withdraw the invaluable £3 a week allowance they had given her from her Trust fund when she joined the Slade.

My family was entranced and delighted with Att from the first moment – they loved her lack of personal vanity, her enthusiasm and single-mindedness and complete lack of 'nonsense', her habit of weeping tears when she laughed helplessly, which she often did. Father was particularly and most gravely interested in her painting, and plied her with respectful questions. He started by painstakingly learning that autumn colours and rich sunsets were not the most valuable ingredients for the prospective picture. When the sun shone low on the elm, F. would say, so timidly, so anxiously 'Att dear – isn't that – *rather* beautiful?'

The Attenboroughs put up a fine wedding party plus a marquee on the lawn. There were strong divergences, right wing and left wing, about the clothes of my contingent. Some of my guests looked rather peculiar against the immaculate cut of my imperturbable brother-in-law, Jack. The Nineteen Seventeener* whom I asked to be an usher was at the height of his stiff clothes-are-nonsense period and arrived in the most stained and shapeless flannel bags of his whole repertoire. Some of these emancipated ones were rather scornful of churches and chapels and the whole ceremony. My best man was Bertie Farjeon [author of revues]. He was subdued and did well: but could not conceal the fact that he had only once been in a church before in his life. When he kneeled, he seemed to collapse on his haunches, in a Moslem attitude. Att wore a red silk dress, something which could be used afterwards. I wore a very new double-breasted suit which in the wedding photograph looks not too well cut. I made a cheeky speech which I was ashamed of for weeks and months afterwards. Then Jack, my brother-in-law, drove us to Dorset in his car, and deposited us, to be by ourselves, while we looked yearningly at his departing figure. We always used to say afterwards, that we enjoyed the rest of our married life all the more because the first

* The 1917 Club was left wing, named in honour of the Russian Revolution.

ten days or so were so extraordinarily testing to our spirits. Having decided to keep our wedding cheque for furniture, we had hit on what we thought was the perfect cheap honeymoon, a spot which turned out uniquely in the end to be both too desolate and too inhabited. Jack Collis [John Stewart Collis, author] had let us have the bottom half of his coastguard cottage on the edge of Chesil Bank. Mile after mile of coast in a straight line of extraordinary grimness – wonderfully brisk and stimulating on a fine day: but we walked into a real Dorset coast mist on our second day. After a melancholy walk along the coast path, I lost Att altogether, for a few minutes, and I had a sudden feeling of panic that she had gone for ever, or that it was a symbol: that I should never keep her for ever.

Now, for the first time in my life, I was caring not flirtingly, or romantically, but absolutely – in love. There had never been the slightest doubt in my wider and deeper consciousness that it must be Att or no one else whatever: though what it was I specially loved about her beyond the perpetual refreshment of her looks, was something I could not say. She was so independent: and her gentle assumption of what she thought was anti-sentimental toughness and ordinariness made her seem exactly the opposite, in my eyes. My only fear was that she didn't love me enough. Did she? I lay in bed looking at her asleep. Fifty yards away the waves were ploughing and gnawing at the shingle. Did she really love me? Really? Really?

God – the gloom of those cottages: and they were not made less gloomy by the other inhabitants. Jack himself was there, in his little room upstairs. He had fallen in love again, deeply and rather tragically this time, because the girl had had to go back to her home in America. Jack sat silent before his untouched typewriter, half eating horrible meals out of tins. The other two cottages were even less cheerful. Middleton Murry was living next door, and was just discovering that his second wife, like his first, was suffering from tuberculosis. The other side Tomlinson, the fine author of *Galleon's Reach*, was recovering, or failing to recover, from the loss of his son, who had drowned in the sea in front of us five weeks before.

But none of these things deeply affected us. To the sound of the waves and the gulls and the swans flying towards Abbotsbury we walked off, blissfully happy when the sun came out, sometimes making love on the shingle, on our bed of pebbles, which seemed as soft as down.

The wedding was described from a different viewpoint in a long and nerve-shattered letter from Att's mother to Stephen's:

I am now beginning to feel a bit rested thank you – it has all been like a dream – so quickly over – the news was announced so suddenly to us – it seemed such a big upheaval all at once – I should not have been surprised to have heard they were *engaged*

– but wanting to be married so soon was a big shock – but all the same was not surprised they would not listen to our advice to wait a year – but I hope all will go well – they seem so suited to each other I think they must be happy.

Lastly the following letter from Att on honeymoon at Chesil Beach to her mother-in-law gives an idea of the less than luxurious style of the honeymoon:

What a lovely lot of things arrived from you this morning. Thank you most awfully. Everything arrived quite safely, except unfortunately the bananas which were smashed as flat as pancakes. Your first hamper was too simply ripping and lasted us for ages – also the jam – unfortunately the strawberry was smashed, but the other two are still going strong.…

CHAPTER 4

OVERLOOKING THE EYOT

At the time when the newly-married Potters were looking for somewhere to live, a number of artists and writers were settling around Hammersmith and Chiswick. The squire of this community was Alan Herbert, the host of the boat-race party, where they had first met. He was now independent MP for Oxford University and more widely known as APH, the contributor to *Punch*. The Herberts owned a number of houses in the area, one of which was now let to the Potters.

No. 2 Riverside was a small eighteenth-century semi-detached. London is full of such houses, but this one was in Chiswick Mall, with a wall-enclosed back garden, a tiny front garden and, through a gate across the road, a river garden that merged with the fluctuating mud and water level of the Thames. Ten yards across the water was Chiswick Eyot, a loofah-shaped island covered with osiers and uninhabited except by swans. Upstream could be seen a stretch of river tapering towards Barnes. The large Georgian window panes allowed the light to flood in, direct or bouncing off the river. Att revelled in the abundance of light and enhanced it by painting all the furniture white and by placing a large mirror above the mantelpiece.

Stephen and Att had plenty to offer, he as author, she as painter. The fact that their only regular income was Stephen's £200 a year as a lecturer at Birkbeck College was not going to stop them living in a style that matched their potential earnings. Stephen describes how they managed to do so:

To start with, our house. We rented a Queen Anne house on Chiswick Mall. Within a year, we were renting a cottage and, because it was 'going to be so useful on holidays and driving Father and Mother around', I had to have a car. How was it done? Answer: rent of house £52 a year. Rates, £12. Cottage, five shillings a week. Car £65, mostly paid for by Father. The house was cheap because it belonged to Alan Herbert: he didn't want to make money out of Att and he wanted the two rooms at the top to be kept for Deacy. Deacy was his old nurse.

Both felt that now was the time to settle down, work hard and have something to show for it. Att had remarkable powers of concentration, and there was little that could distract her once she had set up her easel and made a start. Stephen had more difficulty in settling down. Faced with a copy date, he could if need be work through the night. Without that spur, the rival attractions of golf, squash or tennis; or of botany or other peripheral interests, or of just going for a three-hour walk to get his daily quota of exercise, were all too great.

A more valid impediment to work was lack of space. The first-floor back room at No. 2 Riverside was for a long time filled with the furniture of a previous occupant, Major Bernard Montgomery. Stephen wrote firm letters demanding its removal but was met with an even

Fig. 3 With Stephen in the mirror

firmer refusal to do anything about it. (As Field Marshal, Monty was later to show just how firm he could be.) The top floor was occupied by Deacy. This left only the first-floor front room to serve as living-room, Stephen's study and Att's studio. Stephen describes here the two of them working together:

> During one period we divided the main room into two during the day with a screen and I had plenty of opportunities, round the corner of the screen, of watching Att work. She painted with concentration, screwing up her wide eyelids into a hundred wrinkles. Stepping back from the easel, up to the easel, nearly putting her nose in the paint, her fine self eclipsed by an overall, which carried a thick mosaic of paint smear. At this time Att was concentrating on still life – bloaters and kippers were particularly engaging her. As the days went by, the colours of the fish began to change, sometimes with a faint iridescence.
>
> 'When are you going to get out of your fish period, my dear old darling old sweetheart?' I said. Her overall was beginning to stick out in front a bit, with our child.
>
> 'These fish are changing it's absolutely bloody,' she used to say all in one sentence. Planting her feet still more firmly, squeezing her eyes into slits, she would continue: 'I can't get *away* enough – get *away*'. She turned the canvas upside down. 'You can see the comp better,' she explained.

The composition of *Red Mullet* can be seen in plate 5, with the wrapping paper so arranged as to distance the fish from the snowy background. Their colour has not yet begun to turn.

Stephen describes how sociable neighbours, mostly with children, would spill out onto the street and river gardens. Some thought that if the first-floor window was open, this was as good as an invitation to drop in for a chat. 'Atty – are you at home?' they would call up from the road.

Att painted on through these distractions, but a more serious worry was the dangerously painful birth of her two children. Both births took place in No. 2 Riverside, with Stephen squirting chloroform from an 'instrument like a scent spray' as it was needed. My brother Andrew's weight and broad shoulders caused complications. The doctor was inept – too diffident, according to Stephen, and 'a born non-doctor'. Att was knocked out by the delivery, had a temperature for three weeks afterwards and could not leave her bed. A letter written at that time has the quavery handwriting of the very ill. Soon after she recovered, Andrew became unable to keep his food down and steadily lost weight. The vomiting was 'projectile' and pyloric stenosis was diagnosed. The only cure was to operate and this was done – successfully. But the technique had only just been discovered and the episode caused great anxiety. Three years later, in 1931, I was born, and at 10½ lbs, the birth was not much easier and again there were severe complications. Probably it was decided then that Att would have no more children. Her powers of recuperation were good, but the birth of her two sons dented her stamina.

About this time a living-in nurse was taken on, which meant that now the studio-cum-study-cum-living-room was also used as my parents' bedroom. This arrangement worked well, enabling Att to resume her routine of painting throughout each morning. But her children were not so sure. Aged three, I am reported to have asked: 'Is it true that we have a nurse so that you can paint?' 'Yes darling'. 'Well then, why can't the nurse do the painting?'

The nurse and twice-a-week cook made further inroads on the family finances, but help came from Stephen's family. His father Frank was doing well in the small accountancy firm he worked for in Victoria Street. Later he was brought into partnership, and it was re-named Bird and Potter. He paid for the car and, when the children arrived, he and his wife ('Mother Lilla' to Att) had them down for countless weekends to their Reigate home. Every August, for the entire month, Frank would rent a house at Swanage large enough for the two of them, their maid Minnie, Stephen's sister Muriel (for twenty-six years headmistress of South Hampstead High School for Girls), my parents, my brother and myself. In addition, there was also the weekly food parcel. The main meal of the week was lamb or chicken, sent to Chiswick in a parcel by Mother Lilla. There may have been a lack of variety in the food parcels, as one week she wrote: 'Stephen says may we have beef this week, and cheshire cheese instead of cheddar?' Later, she gets more bold:

> Dearest Mother Lilla. May we have a wild duck this week? Like the chicken, it will do for two or three go's, and a bit of veal, and a *small* bit of mutton for the children – if this doesn't come to too much …

Whatever their money worries, clearly the Potters were not going to starve.

Att completed over a hundred oils and numerous watercolours during her twelve years in Chiswick Mall. There she developed the habit of painting what was to hand, rather than travelling around in search of suitable subjects. Ornaments from the house appeared and recurred in a number of still lifes. The same vases were used in a succession of flower paintings. In *Lilies and Cigar Box* (plate 4) the style is figurative, but without fussy detail, which would in any case have been difficult to include, given the extensive use of a broad palette knife in the application of the paint. Perhaps it was the exclusion of detail that enabled her to highlight essentials, and so add to one's awareness of the objects painted – the texture of the wooden lid, the habit of growth of the flower.

The Window, Chiswick (plate 7), painted in 1929, also demonstrates this ability. The clouds and the almond blossom are each no more than two strokes of the palette knife; the iron gate is quickly sketched in. Close inspection reveals only the ridge marks made by the knife. Yet from three steps back, the scene appears fully depicted; indeed one feels as if one was seeing it clearly for the first time. In *Chrysanthemums* (plate 8), painted a few years later, the inessentials are even sketchier. There is less reliance on the palette knife, and the same round table that appeared in *The Window* is indicated with a rough wash of thinly painted brushwork.

Att painted at least two portraits while at Chiswick, having been persuaded by eager sitters to go back on her earlier resolution to give them up. But her main subject was the misty greys and greens of the Eyot, the mud banks and the river, distanced by a vase of flowers or an ornament on the windowsill. Views through the studio window were to be a constant theme, wherever she was living.

The Window, Chiswick was bought by the Tate after my mother's death and the Gallery, in the plaque below where it hung, stressed her association with the Seven and Five. I queried this, in view of what has already been related about her leaving that group in its early stages. The Keeper of the Modern Collection, Richard Morphet, replied that although she had left the Society early on, the problem was that in its heyday 'leading members such as Hitchens and Ben and Winifred Nicholson developed an approach to subject matter and the use of paint with which it is difficult not broadly to associate your mother's work. Her work shares with theirs an interest in the poetry of simple everyday motifs painted with great freshness and sophisticated simplicity, and also with a delight in the properties of colour and of paint itself. Among the Tate's Potters, both *The Window* and the much later *East Coast Window* are of motifs particularly associated with the Seven and Five in its heyday, so I feel sure that when historians look at the whole sweep of twentieth-century British art they will be bound to notice these kinds of affinity.'

Att's first 'one-man' show was at the Bloomsbury Gallery in 1932. It was respectfully reviewed in the national press. In 1934 she shared an exhibition with Edna Clarke Hall at the Redfern Gallery in Cork Street. The reviews called attention to the subtlety of her colour contrasts and *The Observer* wrote:

> Miss Potter has reduced her palette to a series of flat, greyed tints placed one against another with very subtle oppositions.

As a painter, Att was working in comparative isolation. The only local artist she knew was Gertrude Hermes, the wood engraver and sculptor. She was visited by ex-Slade artists from other parts of London, but Chiswick friends tended to be more literary and political, mostly on the left wing. Every day my brother and I were driven to an avant-garde co-ed in North London by the chauffeur of Dick and Naomi Mitcheson – he was a Labour MP, she a communist writer. Stephen's greatest friend and main golfing opponent, Edgar Lansbury, was the son of the leader of the Labour party. The Lansburys and the Potters had shared a cottage at Berrick Salome, near Nettlebed – until Edgar died of cancer at an intolerably early age. He was the father of the actress, Angela.

Stephen had met Lansbury at the 1917 Club, where he had been a member since before he met Att. He saw it as a 'cheap and intellectually stimulating place for lunch'. Members who now became friends of Att as well as Stephen included Bertie Farjeon, Gerald Barry (future editor of *The News Chronicle* and organiser of the Festival of Britain) and Cyril Joad, whose pedantic voice later became, through *The Brains Trust*, one of the best known in the country.

One member who already knew Att before she met Stephen was Francis Meynell. Francis, as the title of his autobiography *My Lives* indicates, had many different sides. At the 1917 Club, his radical conscience and left-wing views were to the fore. A pacifist in the first world war, he had been sent to prison, but had succeeded in forcing his release by dint of a hunger strike combined with a thirst strike. Between the wars, Francis's main activity was the creation of The Nonesuch Press, where one of his other selves exercised fastidious control over the typography, design, paper and binding of each book. As a result, each product of the Nonesuch was a work of art in itself, and the business flourished.

Francis had met Att at parties and became one of her keenest admirers. He now became a loyal and lasting friend of Stephen as well. From the late 1930s, he was usually accompanied by 'Bay' Kilroy, his wife to be. Bay, who worked at the Board of Trade, had a

Fig. 4 Att

kindly and relaxed manner, masking the brilliance and toughness at work that was to bring her some of the top assignments in her Department.

Francis and Bay saw a great deal of the Potters, both in London and at the remote farmhouse in Essex that belonged to Francis's wife at that time, Vera. For a number of years they also went on holiday together to Talloires, by the Lake of Annecy. Bay, who as Dame Alix Meynell wrote her own autobiography,* recorded the fun of those carefree holidays, when Stephen would send up one of his 'Eng. Lit.' lectures at Birkbeck, Att would come out with one of her songs or together they would mimic a choirboy duet. Bay wrote elsewhere that 'Francis's admiration and affection for Att was unreserved and unclouded'. His first courting present to Bay had been one of Att's early paintings.

Although travelling abroad less, Att and Stephen enjoyed a regular round of weekend visits: to the Booths near Chichester, to Francis and Bay in Essex, to the Lansburys – and to the Nicholses at Lawford Hall, Manningtree. The diplomat Phil Nichols was now married and had inherited this spectacularly beautiful house in Essex, with walled garden, farm and parkland attached. It was the Nicholses who introduced the Potters to Joyce Grenfell; and

* *Public Servant, Private Woman*. Gollancz, 1988.

the Potters who persuaded Joyce to perform at one of their parties where Bertie Farjeon – the revue writer – was a guest. This launched her on her career as an entertainer, as has already been recounted in the autobiographies of Francis, of Bay and of Joyce herself.

After Edgar died, the Potters rented a tumbledown cottage at the foot of the South Downs. The hills were a balm, but two days there meant two days of hard physical work for Att, and the cottage was not used often. More relaxing were visits to Stephen's parents, either to Reigate for the weekend, or to Swanage for the August holiday. At Swanage, with Stephen on the golf course, Minnie to cook and Mother Lilla to sit on the beach with the children, Att had plenty of time to paint – and for me at least her pictures of the sun-baked beach and sea (plate 6) are among her most evocative.

Stephen's parents had only recently moved from Balham to Reigate, which by comparison, was regarded as the country. 'Mother Lilla' accepted Att and was kind to her. But she was a domineering lady and obsessively concerned with the welfare of her grandchildren and son. Her instructions to her daughter-in-law 'never to let Stephen go into a room where there is a smell of paint' were not helpful: the whiff of turps and oil paint permanently pervaded that first-floor room in Chiswick. Att probably got on better with her father-in-law, and painted his portrait. Minnie adored having the children, who sometimes came on their own. So the Chiswick–Reigate route was often taken; and at the same time, Att's visits to Beckenham became less infrequent. Att's parents had come to accept that she was serious about her profession and realised that she was making a success of it. But the couple were still regarded as bohemian and they could not resist playing up to their supposed role. My cousin Gwen Payne described them coming down to Bromley for a formal, full-dress family wedding, with Stephen wearing an open-neck blue shirt. Att teased more gently. Presented on another occasion with a couple of beer mugs, she exclaimed to her teetotal father: 'They will be lovely for *lemonade*'.

So there were opportunities enough to get away from the cramped quarters of No. 2 Riverside, but in fact Chiswick Mall exercised a strong pull, and it was usually a relief to get back home. In those days it may not have been as chic as it is now. It was not so car-dominated either, despite the Potters' acquisition. Coal was delivered from a horse-drawn cart, the ice-cream man came on a bicycle incorporating an Eldorado deep freeze and the muffin man came on foot, tray on head, ringing a bell. There was usually a strong smell of river mud, especially at low tide when, in wellingtons, it was possible to walk across to the Eyot. High tide frequently flowed across the road, making the Mall impassable. In the days when *The Times* ran a single large photograph on its back page every day, it chose once to show Chiswick Mall in full flood. The focus of the picture was a baby in a pram (myself) being inspected by one of the passing swans. On another occasion the river came further than the road, and into the basements of the houses. I was woken to be shown the water rushing through the keyhole of the basement dining-room door and rising up the stairs. Before long the dining-room table was knocking against the ceiling and the fridge in the kitchen had been turned upside down. But this disaster only struck once; and in general this intimacy with the river served to give the Mall a feeling not perhaps of the country, but of something a bit wild, certainly not town.

The twelve years at Chiswick were happy, busy and productive. Stephen's next three books, which included the first biography of D. H. Lawrence, won him praise amongst critics and literary academics, but did not sell in any quantity. In the late 1930s he began to write regularly for the Schools department of the BBC. He also wrote occasional feature programmes, some of which were produced by Mary Allen, Att's friend from the Slade. The BBC money made it possible to build a study at the end of the garden. There Stephen did all his writing and usually slept, so making the living-room more acceptable as a studio for Att. But the real breakthrough did not come for either of them until the beginning of 1939, their last year in Chiswick.

On 18 December 1938, Joyce Grenfell wrote in her *Observer* column (just *before* her introduction to the Potters):

> I hardly dare even whisper the good news in case it all turns out to be a beautiful dream, but it really does look as if the feature programme has swung out of its rut into a wide new spaciousness that leaves one breathless. The man behind this revolution is Stephen Potter … And now comes the glad news that, in January, he is to join the department as a full-time writer and producer.

At the beginning of 1939 Stephen, who like Att was as old as the century, started his first full-time job, in the Drama and Features department of the BBC. At the time he may have regarded this as a set-back, an acceptance of the fact that he was not making an adequate living as a freelance writer. In retrospect, however, it was the start of a productive and successful period in his career.

Meanwhile Att had been offered a one-man show at Arthur Tooth & Son, one of the best of the West End galleries, then in New Bond Street. Since the Bloomsbury Gallery and Redfern shows in 1932 and 1934, she had participated in mixed shows and taken odd pictures to various galleries in the hope that they would sell them for her; but she had had no lasting arrangement with any of them. The offer now made by Richard Smart of Tooths was a triumph and looked like being a turning point. She produced for the show the best of her river scenes (such as *Lily of the Valley by the River*, plate 9) and still lifes. The reviewers wrote of her colour contrasts in terms that could have been, and sometimes were, equally well applied to much of her late work. *The Sunday Times* wrote:

> The mood is emphasised by her unusually delicate sense of the harmony between closely related colours. She can build a picture out of one green and three pale greys, giving each grey its own character, where a less sensitive painter would have muddled them together and lost the quiet interplay between them.

Fig. 5 Stephen

The critics were right to comment on Att's colour and tone contrasts. Although later on her work was to develop and change, she always remained most particular about getting the shade exactly right. It may not be uncommon to be able to recognise, say, Chinese red or Prussian blue, but Att would have in her mind's eye a range for each of these shades. Gwen John, who also had a sharpened sense of colour, resorted to nature in her descriptions: *rouge Phénicien* was 'the colour of the stem of wild geranium', or *cinabre clair* was 'the colour of the little ball holding the snowdrop petals'. So did Att, but she was more down-to-earth. She specified 'pig pink' for an illustration to her school magazine. When asked by Stephen's secretary whether 'donkey brown' adequately described her new coat, she replied 'more cowpat'.

In financial terms the Tooth's show was not momentous. Having sold thirteen paintings she got a cheque some months later from the gallery for £21 1s 10d 'in settlement of the amounts which have been paid for to date …' Nonetheless Att found herself on the map as a widely admired artist. That and Stephen's new job made the Potters confident enough to raise a mortgage for a house of their own, and in the spring of 1939 they moved from No. 2 Riverside to Thames Bank, a few doors along the Mall.

Thames Bank was a bigger house, and all of it belonged to the Potters. There was a drive and garage, a large garden with a walled-off area for vegetables, and enough room for a studio and study. At last Att had the space and seclusion she needed. All seemed set for a long and fruitful working partnership – but for the threat of war. Stephen wrote in his diary: 'We have been in the new house for a week – lovely freedom and space – it is heaven – only shadow, thought of possible bombs.' When war broke out, only six months after they had moved in, Stephen told Att: 'Don't cry. Whatever happens now, we've had a wonderful life.'

CHAPTER 5

NOT A
'WAR ARTIST'

When war was declared, we were in a cottage in Worth Matravers, a few miles inland from Swanage. An hour after Chamberlain's broadcast, Stephen said a solemn goodbye to all of us and left for the Drama and Features department, which had already been evacuated from London to Evesham. There, on top of a heavy work programme, he set about trying to find somewhere for Att and me; but with an influx to the town of 300 BBC staff and other refugees from London, this was no easy task. Att soon went up to help him – full of foreboding about where we would live. She wrote twice from Evesham to Richard Smart of Tooth's, first from the Northwick Arms Hotel on 18 September:

> I have come up here to keep house for Stephen and one child. We hope to share with several people in a house outside the town, but now all plans are wrecked by the possibility of the whole department being moved somewhere else! Stephen is lucky to have a comparatively safe job ... At the same time his other sources of income vanish and we are reduced to exactly half, with the Chiswick house on our hands. Now *how* does one cash in on the job of painting the generals, and pictures of hospitals and so on?

Att wrote again on 9 October, from lodgings decorated with aspidistras and texts on the walls:

> People keep telling me that now is the time for cheap people like me to come out with a splash, as all valuable work has been put away. I wonder what will happen really. I shouldn't have thought a thing would ever be sold. The latest news here is that we have got to go and live in Manchester. It's really too foul for words.

The threatened move took place on 16 November; but by then Att was back at Thames Bank, partly in an attempt to sell it and partly in order to prepare six small paintings for an exhibition at the Leicester Galleries, to be held at the end of the month. She then went to fog-bound Manchester to look for lodgings. Her base was a pub, where she was glad to find her Slade friend Mary Allen, now a high-powered BBC executive, also looking for accommodation.

All BBC staff were in the same boat. Before long the Potters had linked up with friends and friends of friends, to share a fair-sized house in Platt Lane. It was overlooking a park, about fifteen minutes by bus from the centre. The persisting core of this household was Stephen, Att, Laurence Gilliam (Stephen's boss as Head of Features) and Marianne Helweg, Laurence's intended wife. Valentine Dyall (then famous for his deep and sinister voice as 'the Man in Black') and his wife-to-be Babette left after a few weeks, possibly because Babette was the loser in the discussion as to whether she or Att should have the one room suitable as a studio. In the course of this struggle, she was heard to say 'Att is ludicrously overrated as a painter. She just sits there and paints out of the window. She should paint with her *soul*.' Other occupants were Mary Allen, Maurice Brown (a BBC musical advisor) and his wife Thea, and Robert Eddison, a young actor who by 1939 had already played Oberon and other parts on the London stage. Robert only stayed for two months, before being called up as a naval rating. He took with him a lasting fondness for Att, and wrote of her forty-seven years later: 'She had a sort of gravity which, with her capacity for fun too, moved me very much.' During the war they corresponded and her letters, said Eddison, 'lit up my time on the lower deck'.

Work and social life were totally intermixed and there was the occasional tense scene. But the Potters were there for fifteen months, and on the whole the arrangement worked well. As with many people in the early part of the war, the hectic level of the work and the uncertainty of the future produced an atmosphere of exhilaration. Although surrounded by actors, whose main conversational gambit seemed to be telling stories in a variety of local accents, Att held her own. She acted Stephen making the bed by holding the two corners upright, then falling flat on his face to get it straight across the bed. She imitated Laurence slowly uncoiling his weighty body before dealing with an impertinent question.

The growing danger of air-raids increased the camaraderie. The household frequently had to eat and sleep in the cellar. The issue of *Picture Post* of 15 March 1941 featured 'The BBC at War' and included two pages of photographs of the ménage, sharing meals and working in tin hats. If sleep in the cellar was impossible, Robert Eddison would rehearse one of his parts in this crowded retreat. Both Stephen and Att had to take turns as fire-watchers, and one of Stephen's most dangerous wartime acts was to extinguish an incendiary bomb with his foot.

Rations were shared and a cooking roster was organised. Robert's spaghetti bolognese went down particularly well – otherwise, the men were absolved. Among the women, there may have been a slight feeling that while they were doing important war work with the BBC, Att was the only one not to have a 'serious' job – and indeed if because of some crisis Mary Allen (or whoever) did not get back till midnight on her day to cook, obviously someone else had to do it.

One boost for Att at this tumultuous time was the purchase by the Tate of its first Mary Potter, *Golden Kipper* (plate 10). This must have been painted immediately after the move to Manchester, at the very end of 1939. In a 1958 letter to Martin Butler of the Tate, she tells him it was painted in Manchester in 1940. However, it was exhibited in a United Artists exhibition at the Royal Academy that began on 5 January, so there would hardly have been time to paint it in that year. Another curiosity about the painting is that unbeknown to anyone except Att, the Academy had hung it on its side. Nonetheless Raymond Mortimer enthused about it in his *New Statesman* review and picked it out (among 2,218 exhibits) as 'much the most charming in the show'. Att put down her good fortune to the salesmanship of Richard Smart.

Richard had become an unquenchable supporter and encouraged Att to carry on painting despite all difficulties. In the summer of 1940 he organised a mixed show of new work by nine artists, including Augustus John, Paul Nash, Matthew Smith, Stanley Spencer – and Mary Potter. However there is no record of any sales from this show, although she did sell three in the earlier 'little pictures' exhibition at the Leicester Galleries.

Att's work while at 66 Platt Lane was perhaps more restricted than at any other time. The only painting from her window traced so far is plate 11, which shows the view from the house into the park – foggy as usual. The only still life, a vase of violets, which was bought by J. B. Priestley (a frequent visitor to the house) as a present for Mary Allen. She did at least three portraits and that of Mary Allen herself, alert as a bird, can be seen in fig. 6. From time to time she sent a picture up to Richard, which he usually managed to sell. But she fretted that her domestic chores took up far too much of the day.

Another worry was the bombing. Att had spent part of September 1940 back in London, in another forlorn attempt to sell Thames Bank. Air raids on the capital had started, but Att continued for a few days to stay on in the house, even after its windows had blown in. Soon after her return to Manchester, the blitz started in earnest there and reached its peak just before Christmas, when my brother and I returned home for the holiday. She took us to stay at a pub, the Bird in Hand, just outside the city and comparatively safe. On the nights of 22 and 23 December, the whole of central Manchester was set alight by a long rain of fire bombs. Stephen was up at the BBC both nights, organising a team of fire watchers, and dodging through the flaming streets between the various BBC blocks. On the day of the 23rd he and the BBC 'rep' somehow contrived to produce a programme about the discovery of an historical document with marginal notes written by Shakespeare. He had difficulty in getting back to the Bird in Hand on Christmas Eve because the roads were choked with refugees.

After the blitz and Christmas the family returned briefly to Platt Lane; but they did not

Fig. 6 Portrait of Mary Allen

intend to stay. Stephen wrote in his diary: 'In general, a year slightly too social, though amusingly social, makes us long to be on our own'. Moreover the bombing continued and often prevented him from making the short journey back home from the BBC. The Potters lost confidence in the family's immunity to air raids. Att's resolve to go on painting, war or no war, hardened. The decision to quit was taken in February 1941, when Att wrote to Mother Lilla:

> I am the only cook at the moment, as Thea Brown is at Berkhamsted, as her child there is ill, and Marianne Gilliam is having a holiday. I have given my month's notice! We leave here in 3 weeks time. As yet we haven't found anywhere to go to. I *must* get on with my work, and make some money quickly. It is quite ridiculous spending all my time cooking for the BBC.

After leaving Platt Lane, rooms were found in Hale, a suburb to the south, in country described by Stephen in his diary as 'low, flat and misty and fairly built over, but good Sussex compared to Manchester'. A great bonus of Hale was the proximity of the Simpson family. Ronald (Ronnie) Simpson was in the BBC Rep., and had parts in most of Stephen's programmes. The Simpsons lived in an elegant house outside Mobberley, which was within bicycling distance. Their croquet lawn kept Andrew and me out of the way for much of the holidays. Most wonderful of all, in exchange for one of Att's pictures, Ronnie lent the Potters his tiny and ancient Austin 7, so enabling Stephen to get down most evenings from the BBC to Red Arch, as our home was called.

The lodgings at Hale were comfortable and the landlady grudgingly allowed Att to paint in the sitting-room, which at least during the term-time she was able to do. Despite complaints about untidiness and constant worries about getting paint on carpets and chaircovers, Att produced many new works during the ten-month stay at Hale. They were mostly taken up to London by Stephen, who had to go there most weeks anyway, as the Drama and Features department was moving in stages back to the capital. He visited Tooth's on 23 May, only to find it wrecked by a bomb – only the walls remained, 'tottering in mud'. (Two of Att's paintings were found under the rubble: they were undamaged.) Tooth's being *hors de combat*, Att exhibited four pictures in another mixed show at the Leicester Galleries; and two in a London Group exhibition in the Léger Galleries. 'Badly hung in poky gallery', wrote Stephen. 'P's pictures somewhat killed by tough, slick Laura [Knight].' Stephen was soon dismissed as a courier after absent-mindedly leaving two other pictures on the train.

Two years into the war and still not commissioned to paint generals, Att again felt she ought to paint something military, as is revealed in this August 1941 letter from the War Artists' Advisory Committee (WAAC):

> Dear Mrs Potter,
>
> Mr Gatehouse has handed me your letter to him of 6 August, in which you ask if you could get permission to go into Tatton Park to sketch parachutists.
>
> I put your request to the Artists' Advisory Committee at their meeting yesterday at which the Service representatives were present and we found that the subject that you wish to sketch is forbidden. The Committee however would like to assist you if

there are any other subjects of a less inaccessible kind for which you would like to have facilities, and I hope you will let me know if there is anything we can do for you in that way.

Perhaps I should explain that the red sketching permit which you possess, while it entitles you to include in your sketches 'prohibited objects', does not entitle you to work in 'protected places', such as aerodromes and coastal defence areas. For the latter you must secure special permission from the Service or Services concerned, and a good way to set about doing this is to write to me as Secretary of WAAC.

Yours sincerely,

EM O'R Dickey

This letter is quoted in full not because it explains, but because it touches on the mystery of why Att was not included in the 300-strong list of 'War Artists' patronised by the Ministry of Information. Lists of artists were drawn up by the WAAC, of which O'R Dickey, seconded from the Ministry, was the all-powerful secretary. Kenneth Clark was the chairman: it was only later that he was to enthuse about Mary Potter's paintings. The WAAC did a good job in ensuring that British artists were able to continue working during the war and the superb selection of their paintings in the Imperial War Museum today demonstrates the success of their efforts. But if not on the list it was, according to Alan Ross in *Colours of War*, virtually impossible for artists to operate. Ministry of Information purchases were put on show around the country and many a reputation was built in this way, with the subsequent benefit of private and public commissions. Att was excluded not because she was a woman (a few female artists were on the list), but more probably because of the peaceful, unemphatic nature of her work. And in spite of the 'red sketching permit' referred to in the letter, nothing in all her output can be found, except for one portrait, that is remotely related to the war.

On hearing that Stephen's department was moving down to London, Att's first reaction was one of relief; but she had, in her two years at Manchester, developed links which she was sorry to break. The City Art Gallery had acquired two of her paintings and the Curator, Lawrence Howard, wrote to her: 'And is it true that you are leaving Manchester? It seems the fate of all the people we should like to keep here to be whisked off to London as soon as they have taken root and made Mancunians want them.'

When the Potters finally moved south, however, they chose to live not in London, but in a farmhouse in Essex. This may have been because of the continued bombing of the capital, or may simply have been due to the unexpected offer of a large house, near friends, at an affordable rent. Berwick Hall was two miles from Francis Meynell's house (Bradfields), where Stephen and Att had continued to go for occasional weekends, even from Manchester. The Potters' new home was owned by Dick – later Sir Leslie – Plummer, who was then Managing Editor of the *Daily Express*. Dick also lived two miles off, in a house called Hoses. Stephen and Att had spent a long weekend at Hoses in November, during which she painted Dick's portrait while Stephen inspected and mulled over the pros and cons of Berwick Hall. He was attracted to it mainly by the unspoilt though desolate countryside. 'So we now get the rambling country house I most wanted after all', he wrote.

They moved in December. To begin with Att had to concentrate on getting the house straight. It was extremely cold and the Plummers and Francis and Bay preferred to offer constant hospitality in the evenings, rather than sit shivering as the guests of the Potters. Stephen was digging clods of frozen earth 'the size of fenders' and Att claimed that on one occasion the hot-water bottle froze solid in her bed. But by the end of February Stephen was writing: 'Wind still in the North and some snow – but P. and I are ecstatic together in this divine house'. Att was to spend the remaining three-and-a-half years of the war there, usually on her own during the week, but with Stephen down from London at weekends and with Andrew and me around during the holidays.

The farmhouse was remote indeed – half a mile from the two-shop village of Toppesfield, four miles from the station and nine from the nearest town, Halstead. These places were reached by bicycle, as there was no longer a car. Contact with Dick or with Francis and Bay (both then in the Board of Trade) was at weekends only, but the three-way links that were formed undoubtedly saved Att from feeling too shut off; and at least Dick's wife – Beattie – was usually at home during the week. Sometimes she would drive Att into Halstead in search of luxuries such as gin, not available at the village stores.

There was a remarkable contrast between the stateliness of Berwick Hall outside, and the lack of comforts inside. The long, lime-lined drive to the pillared gateway can be seen in a number of Att's paintings; the grounds included a fruit and vegetable garden and a small lake. The french windows of the drawing-room led onto a terrace, below which was a lawn only just shorter than the regulation size for croquet and we quickly brought it up to standard. The banister rail of the oak staircase was nearly a foot across, and rose from an empty hall which was itself nearly as big as the whole of the ground floor of No. 2 Riverside. The other side of the coin was that there was no electricity or gas, drinking water came from an outside pump and inside, other water had to be pumped upstairs. It was a windy house, and would have been impossible to keep warm, even if coal had not been rationed. Food was probably not quite such a problem as for people living in towns, but even so Att had to scratch around. One Friday evening when Stephen had arrived by bicycle from the station, she told him that for a vegetable she had found a tin of Fortnum & Mason spinach. Not until he had finished his dinner did he learn that he had been eating stinging nettles.

Long term, Att's career was well served by the Berwick Hall period, since there she had plenty of opportunity to work and she stored up many paintings for exhibition later. As ever, she painted the view from her studio window. Plate 12, showing both studio and the already-mentioned pillared gateway, is unusual in that the view takes second place to the interior. She painted still lifes. She painted the Essex countryside. But, with the exception of three pictures in a 1943 London Group exhibition, the only place during the Berwick Hall years where her new work was exposed to the public was the British Restaurant at Halstead. British Restaurants, which were subsidised, offered a reasonable meal for less than a shilling. The Ministry of Works thought it would improve public morale to make them less drab, and commissioned Kenneth Clark's wife Jane, on a shoestring budget of £300, to get paintings up on their walls. Some were done by students; some were lent free by the artists. Some British Restaurant walls were found not suitable for the hanging of pictures and artists were found to paint murals. Att worked flat out for three weeks, covering a wall.

Short term, Att's star was nearing obscurity. She was not asked to participate in the 'Recording Britain' project – the Pilgrim Trust was commissioning artists to build up a record of all parts of the country as they looked at the time. Nor did she win the patronage of the Council for the Encouragement of Music and the Arts (CEMA). This body, later to evolve into the Arts Council, had begun buying contemporary paintings which it then sent around the country on touring exhibitions. She was reconciled to not being a War Artist, but depressed when two pictures she had submitted to CEMA were not bought.

The only paintings that Att sold from Berwick Hall were portraits – mostly of friends. Phil Nichols asked her to paint his daughters Anne and Jo-Jo, with Lawford Hall in the background. Of another picture, Stephen recorded in his diary J. B. Priestley's comments: 'Att's portrait of Pete's little girl. It is one of the most beautiful portraits I have seen. She has the gift as no-one I know of making a good portrait a good picture.' Att also painted Francis, Bay (fig. 7), Beattie – and Beattie's niece, wearing a sergeant's uniform. This was her one war-related picture. (It was not until 1994 that the Imperial War Museum tracked it down and bought it.)

Helpful as these commissions were, Att did not enjoy them and complained to Stephen: 'I am sick of painting portraits, staring at the shadow under the nose'. Periodically she would rebel against portrait painting, which she found exhausting and limiting. Even friends, however tactful, were apt to ask for minor changes in this feature or that; and Att disliked having to make the lower lip smaller, or enlarge the right eye. But none of this detracts from her skill in revealing the character of the sitter and her ability to combine 'a good portrait' with 'a good picture'.

Att's portraits were much admired in her own corner of Essex; but without a wider platform, it must have been at the back of her mind that the reputation so well bolstered by the Tooth's show in 1939 was in danger of disappearing. In answer to Sir John Rothenstein, who as director of the Tate had written asking for a list of what she considered to be her best pictures, she wrote: 'I have not yet set the Thames on fire with anything, as far as the public is concerned'. One of her sitters was her sub-tenant, Ethel Fry. Stephen wrote in his diary:

> Last train home. P. is painting a picture of Mrs Fry which no-one will see and she has such a marvellous line in portraits – dear dear *dear* she should be a war artist. Much more of an artist than I am, she has had the greatest bad luck in not being followed up more at the moment.

It was fortunate that Att's protagonist and chief salesman Richard Smart had kept in touch with her throughout the war, encouraging her to continue painting with the promise of another show when it was over.

Fig. 7 Portrait of Bay

CHAPTER 6

HARLEY STREET

Although Phil Nichols wrote to Att from Prague, '… do not forget that you are going to take a house eventually near Lawford', it had always been taken for granted that, as soon as the war was over, a family home would again be found in London. In Manchester and in Essex, my parents had thought of themselves as being in exile. The BBC was in London and so were the galleries, with whose co-operation Att now hoped to take up a less interrupted career. Moreover Andrew and I were both now at Westminster School, which had returned from evacuation in the country in 1945, and where we were now going to be dayboys.

So London it was – nothing semi-rural like Chiswick, but in the middle of town, a flat in No. 135 Harley Street. Perhaps it was taken in reaction to the too inconveniently deep countryside around Berwick Hall. For Stephen it was within walking distance of the BBC and his club – the Savile. The flat was rented from a fellow Savilian, who was a lung specialist. The gloom of a high-ceilinged, pillared hall was to some extent counteracted by a brightly coloured Mark Gertler, opposite the reception desk. A long climb took you past consulting rooms to the second floor and the first Potter-occupied room, a large drawing-room-cum-dining-room, at the back of the house. On the third floor was the main bedroom and Att's studio, looking east over the street. Next door there was a bombed site, and from the street it always seemed to me as if my bedroom, on the fourth floor, was slightly leaning into the gap in the terrace.

The first major event of the Harley Street years was Att's one-man show in June and July 1946. It was again at Tooth's, which had now found new premises in Bruton Street. Richard Smart convinced Att that her war paintings were the best she had yet produced and orchestrated the show well. He sold over half, which was good for that time of austerity. He wrote: 'The show was a success even if we didn't sell *Rising Moon* – the only real disappointment. Who knows even yet?' Buyers included the National Gallery of New South Wales and the Ministry of Works.

All save two of the pictures had been painted in Essex and depicted wistfully the bleak Essex countryside – grey skies, falling leaves, furrowed fields – or the stillness of trees heavy with snow. *Rising Moon*, a magically beautiful scene, showing Toppesfield church and the entrance pillars and long drive of Berwick Hall (plate 13), was bought in December by the Ferens Art Gallery, Hull – Richard had always had a reliable eye for which pictures were likely to sell. The two post-war paintings, *Doves at the Zoo* (plate 14) and *Picnic*, were both scenes from nearby Regent's Park. The critics were in favour, but with a hint of qualification: Eric Newton's review in *The Sunday Times* was typical:

> Mary Potter, who is holding a one-man show at Tooth's in Bruton Street, shares with
> Frances Hodgkins, Elizabeth Morris and Winifred Nicholson a quality that has never
> been satisfactorily analysed – the quality of femininity. Many women artists lack it,
> and are none the worse for lacking it; others have it in abundance, and are ruined by
> it. But for these four it is the central fact of their painterly style. In Frances Hodgkins's
> case it amounts to positive genius. With Mary Potter it is something less than that,
> but it is also something more than an amalgam of tenderness and charm, though these
> are the qualities in her work that leap to the eye.

Echoing the pre-war reviews, Newton's comment on her palette was:

> She can state with the utmost precision the relationship between tones and colours
> that, to the average casual eye, are almost indistinguishable. She can build her picture
> on a contrast between a pale grey-green, and an equally pale blue-grey.

Meanwhile the developments in Stephen's career were having their effect on Att's. It was during the late 1940s that he became a celebrity. While his writing had always had an ironic bite, his series of 'How' programmes (*How to give a party*, *How to go to the theatre*, *How to blow your own trumpet*, etc), written jointly with Joyce Grenfell, were starting him on a new career as a satirist. The Third Programme was launched in 1946, and to show that it was not going to be exclusively solemn, its very first transmission was *How to Listen*. Then, early in 1947, came the record cold winter and the fuel crisis. Light and heating restrictions forced many office blocks, including the Third Programme, to close down. Stephen, at home for a fortnight with nothing to do, wrote *Gamesmanship*. The success of this book and its sequels was soon to make Stephen into the reference point and final authority on ploys and gambits played out all over the country. Wodges of letters arrived each day, with requests for advice or with new ideas for 'the art of winning games without actually cheating'. Telephone callers asked him to speak at dinners, participate in discussions or write articles. Apart from all this and his regular BBC work, he was for most of this period doing a weekly review of books for *The News Chronicle* and weekly theatre reviews for *The New Statesman*. He was, more than ever before, extremely busy, and much of his work was conducted from home. Stephen's secretary at the BBC, Betty Johnstone, helped with some of this extracurricular activity, but inevitably Att too got landed with peripheral jobs. Manuscripts had to be rushed from A to B, and only she was available to do it. When she was alone in the house, it was she who had to take the telephone calls and deliver the messages. No doubt she shared the pleasure and excitement of Stephen's success. But years later Betty Johnstone described how these tasks, coming on top of household chores, took up a great deal of Att's time and interfered with her main work.

In 1948 Stephen was offered the editorship of *The Leader*, a Hulton Press weekly magazine that was heading for extinction. It was thought that a new editor and a change of direction might save it. Stephen rashly accepted the offer and gave notice to the BBC. He did indeed transform the magazine but by the end of 1949 it was still losing £1,000 a week and Stephen, to his great relief, was asked to leave. He decided to set up as a freelance author. He had ideas for short stories and a play; he had his book and theatre reviews; he would finish a sequel to *Gamesmanship*. As in the 1930s, he was once again working from home.

There were other distractions. In February 1947 Andrew was rushed to hospital with suspected polio. He recovered, but slowly, after many weeks at home. Att herself, who had had at least one post-natal operation in the 1930s, was operated on twice while at Harley Street, the second time for an emergency hysterectomy. Then there were the household chores, the cooking and worst of all, the shopping. The war may have ended, but rationing was as stringent as ever. The best part of a morning could be lost standing in queues in Marylebone High Street.

These difficulties could not be helped; but it was Att's own choice to spread her energies further by taking on two commissions outside her normal field. She had always had a flair for decorating a house, and her friends would consult her about their curtains, carpets or whatever. Now she was invited by the organisers of an exhibition sponsored jointly by the Central Institute of Art and Design and the wallpaper industry to design and furnish a bedroom, with no expense spared and no worries about clothing coupons for the furnishing fabrics. She quickly said yes, enjoyed the task and for once was unstintingly enthusiastic about the result of her own work. The second venture was for Beatrice (Bobo) Mayor, whom Att had got to know at Omonville. Bobo asked Att to design the jacket of her volume of verse, *Voices from the Crowd*. Att produced a one-colour design that exactly fitted the subject – vague dots representing the crowd, and the word 'Voices' emerging from the deep plum background. But she had not expected the amount of technical work, with visits to and from the printer, that her apparently simple and spontaneous design would involve; and she did not seek any more commissions in that field for the time being.

So for one reason or another, Att painted fewer pictures than she had in Essex, and many of them were sold by Richard Smart as and when they were produced. So she took a long time to build up enough for her next show at Tooth's, which was now chalked in for 1951 or 1952. She did however exhibit at the Redfern Gallery in 1949, when one room was set aside for Mary Potter watercolours. For outdoor scenes, Att's method of work was to use watercolour sketches done *in situ* as notes for oil paintings to be worked up later in her studio. They were not primarily intended for mounting and framing; but sometimes she found that she had, on a small scale, created just as effective a picture as had been planned for the finished oil. The immediacy and freshness of these watercolours was admired and it was probably Rex Nan Kivell, a director of the Redfern, who encouraged her to exhibit them.

One of Richard's occasional sales from the gallery was to the National Gallery of Victoria in Melbourne, which bought an oil of pink peonies (plate 15). As in Chiswick days, flowers on the sill backed by the view through the window were again a favourite subject. Somehow she was able to make the opposite side of Harley Street, particularly when the chimneys could be only dimly seen through the smog, as interesting a background as had been the Chiswick Eyot. Regent's Park was two hundred yards up the road from No. 135 and plate 16 shows one of many park scenes. A gardener is sweeping up the leaves in pink-tinged mist – often in those days the sun struggled to get through and remained red all day.

Despite the proximity of Regent's Park, Att was beginning to feel shut in by Harley Street. Uncharacteristically, she went out of her way to find other scenes to paint. With Stephen, she drove in 1946 to the northeast coast of Scotland to paint Eric Linklater's two boys. Portrait commissions, although they meant up to a week in the house of the sitter, at least got her away to new places. Next year, among five portraits undertaken, one was of Mrs John Mills, whose husband invited her to return and paint from his Richmond home, while another of Phyllis Lutyens led to a number of visits with Stephen to the Lutyens's house in Norfolk, designed by her husband's father, Sir Edward. She also painted artist John Armstrong's children in that year, and followed this up with a week at Portmeirion at the home of his estranged wife.

Of all these searchings for new views to paint, much the most successful were Att's visits to Brighton, where friends had pressed her to use their flat as a base for painting as often as she wished. Her watercolours and oils of the rainswept pink paving stones and churning green seas (plate 17), that were the fruit of this hospitality, captured the feeling of Brighton in winter and were snapped up by public galleries or private buyers all too quickly – Richard sold eleven Brighton oils to his Tooth's customers.

Occasional family holidays and weekends away also took Att out of town during her six-and-a-half years in Harley Street but they were not productive as far as painting was concerned. At the end of the war Francis and Bay set up a new home at Cobbolds Mill in mid Suffolk and the Potters were invited many times to stay. One such weekend spanned their wedding night. All four of us were included in the house party. Att drew a mock-rococo cupid in the visitors' book, with two hearts pierced by his arrow. We all solemnly signed this page, as if our signatures were helping to seal the ceremony.

In 1947 we went with the Simpsons to Aldeburgh, on the east coast. They had often sailed there, were buying and converting a derelict cottage off the town steps and wanted to introduce the Potters to the offbeat charm of the town – a resort all but deserted by holidaymakers, not in the least picturesque, and busy with its own preoccupations. It had miles of empty pebble beaches on either side and a hinterland of deserted marsh and heath. Compared to sunny Swanage, the weather was wet and cold. Yet the town appealed to Att and she arranged to stay there again, in a flat belonging to Thea Brown (a former co-occupant of 66 Platt Lane), with a view to painting seascapes for her next show.

By 1949, the flat was beginning to pall and not even the Mark Gertler in the hall could dispel the hushed hospital atmosphere of consulting rooms. Att's gloom was not helped by Stephen's frequent absences – not always on matters connected with his work. Too often he did not return until the small hours of the morning and the silence at the breakfast table was sometimes oppressive. He had always been flirtatious and had had various affairs, at least some of which are recorded in his diary. For him, it was an open marriage. Yet it was a marriage that in other respects appeared to be working well. Occasional quarrels were soon patched up with hugs and kisses. Tender and affectionate references to 'P' continued to appear in Stephen's diaries at this time – and indeed in subsequent years. In February 1948, when he had been ill, he rhapsodises for two pages on the pleasures of being nursed by her. Yet in this same year he first met Heather Jenner, owner of the Bond Street marriage bureau. An affair developed, and although it may not have occurred to either of them that it would eventually break up both their marriages, it now began to undermine the partnership that my parents had achieved. Att wanted a fresh start in a new home.

By the beginning of 1950 there was no necessity to go on living in London. Stephen had left *The Leader*, Andrew was at Oxford and I was doing my national service in Korea. Visits to galleries and publishers alike could be made during brief visits to town, and the Potters began to think of moving to somewhere less pointedly urban. They wanted to buy a house: they were both fifty, yet apart from the brief Thames Bank interlude just before the war, had never done so. During the year, the money became available to make this once again a practical possibility. Firstly, Stephen's freelance status was working out well, as *Lifemanship*, the first sequel to *Gamesmanship*, was an immediate success. Then on Christmas Day his mother died. Her house was put on the market and fetched more than expected. Stephen and Att decided they could afford a house of their own, costing anything up to £6,000.

Att at once set about house hunting. I have detailed documentation of the search, since both parents wrote to me once a week in Korea, and often the news was of hopes or disappointments on the house front. Att looked at houses in Hampstead; she considered a house near Twickenham. She looked in Wallingford, she looked in Marlow. Then in May she found a Queen Anne house with tennis court in Stanwell which she thought ideal, the only snag being that it was between the vicarage and the church and she was worried about being dragooned into attending services. Stephen was now in the States on a five-week lecture tour, but he had left Att a blank cheque for the deposit on the Stanwell house if she decided it was the right thing to do. The seller dropped £1,000 and she was all set to exchange contracts when she found out that a new runway was being built at Heathrow, the noise from which would make Stanwell unacceptable. She withdrew. She went back to Aldeburgh, for the third time in 1951, to paint and await Stephen's return. When he arrived at the beginning of June, Aldeburgh was at its best and for the first time it occurred to them that they might live there. They went round to an estate agent, were shown a house the next day – and decided to buy it.

The Potters began moving into their new home, The Red House, later that summer; but they did not finally abandon Harley Street until the end of November 1951, as Att wanted to keep all her pictures in London until after her next show, now arranged for October – not at Tooth's, but at the Leicester Galleries.

Att's previous one-man show had been in 1946, an uncomfortably long time ago. Three foretastes of her current work had been on view in public galleries since then. The first was in 1949, when the Arts Council organised a show of recent acquisitions of the Contemporary Art Society and included one of the Brighton paintings, *Deserted Pier*. Secondly, in March 1950, an exhibition from the private collections of CAS members was presented at the Tate. For this, Mike Harrison lent an Aldeburgh seascape. Lastly, to coincide with the Festival of Britain in 1951, the Arts Council arranged a large exhibition, 'British Painting 1925–50', at the New Burlington Galleries in London and subsequently at the Manchester City Art Gallery. Att was glad of these opportunities to display her best work to a wider public. She noted with a combination of disapproval and satisfaction that of the fifty-two artists in the 1951 exhibition, which was intended as an international showcase for current British painting, only three were female. Three Mary Potters were hung: one of Regent's Park and two of Brighton.

All this was useful: but another one-man show was imperative, if Att's career was not to lose its momentum. As late as the beginning of 1951, a firm date had not been settled. She wrote to me in February, saying:

> Not much news from London, as I don't seem to have done anything but work for my show. One rather nice thing, the Leicester Galleries wrote and asked me to have a show with them next year, but of course I had to refuse, as I am bound to Tooth's – but it is rather nice, because as they are now so keen on my work, I feel I can fall back on them if anything happened to Tooth's.

Either she was very lucky, or someone had had some advance information. Only three weeks later I had another letter:

> I had a fearful blow by being told last Sat. by Richard Smart that he was leaving Tooth's, as he is fed up with the whole picture business and wants a change – so I will not have a show or picture there any more, as the modern side, for which he alone is responsible, will cease to exist. However, everything ended well, because I dashed along to the Leicester, and they received me with open arms, and will give me a show as soon as possible, probably October, *and* will have a picture or two of mine there all the time.

Thus a switch of galleries was effected painlessly. The Leicester Galleries October show included three Brighton and three Aldeburgh oils, as well as many Harley Street and Regent's Park paintings. The critics were yet again coolly in favour. '… Mrs Mary Potter, a sensitive painter who knows her limitations …' Or *The Times*: 'In her more successful works, and particularly in *Aldeburgh Stones*, she achieves an admirable effect by the use of extremely delicate gradations with here and there a note of just sufficiently unexpected colour …' Such words were not going to make the show a sell-out and were faint praise indeed for the daringly sketchy but perceptive Brighton pictures or the poetry of paintings such as *Peonies*, which have stood the test of time and are still highly regarded by the Galleries that bought them. The show was nonetheless reasonably successful, and was the first of many put on by the Leicester Galleries.

As soon as it was dismantled, the Potters moved to Aldeburgh.

CHAPTER 7

THE RED HOUSE

The seasons in Aldeburgh always seem to be about three weeks later than in the rest of the country. This may have something to do with the retarding effect of the sea on changes in land temperature, but whatever the reason, the fact is that east coast Easters are usually bitterly cold and unpleasant, while autumns linger on, with sunbeams flooding sideways across flat fields into leaves that should have fallen weeks earlier. The skyscapes, with the low horizons and the reflection of the sea, are larger and more light-filled than elsewhere: as in Holland across the water, they have always attracted artists. It was at such a time of year that the Potters moved, in 1951, to Aldeburgh; and after the early winter fog of Harley Street, the contrast in light was striking.

The new home, The Red House, was alongside the fourteenth hole of the golf course. The town was five minutes by car and the sea, which could just be seen from the first floor, a mile away. Its distant glint reflecting the morning sun can be seen in a number of the early Aldeburgh paintings; while a favourite subject from a north window was to be the golf course. Plate 19 shows parties of golfers trudging through the rain, their multicoloured umbrellas softened by the mist.

It was a new start for the Potters. Stephen expected to live there half the week only, as although he had no regular job, his reviews, articles and speaking engagements usually meant going up to town – and in any case, he was not yet prepared to give up Club life and the other attractions of London. Att on the other hand was going to be in Aldeburgh all the time, and enjoyed getting the inside of The Red House exactly as she wanted it. Dark-green Regency stripes in the dining-room, to offset two silver candlesticks. Pompeian red in the drawing-room, as background to the mahogany and gold-coloured clock on the mantelpiece and contrasting with the white-painted bookcases. For another room a stoical decorator managed to come up with a mixture that was nearly right when she asked for a yellow that matched 'the pale daffodils at the end of the lawn when the sun shines through them from the other side'.

The existing gardener was kept on and, as an extravagant innovation, a living-in housekeeper was employed. The theory was that this would leave more time for painting; and that the good working environment for both of them would make it possible to earn enough to support the new lifestyle. A room with mainly north-facing windows was selected as a studio and now at last Att, away from the distractions of London, felt she had the conditions to enable her to concentrate full time on her vocation.

Hours of work varied, but the normal pattern was a full morning's painting in the studio, sometimes to be followed by a second stint after tea. In the afternoons she would rest, play tennis or go for a walk or Suffolk-exploring expedition; sometimes she would decide to continue working outdoors, driving off with sketch pad, watercolours and camp stool. The last jobs of the day, at about 6 pm in summer or with the end of daylight in winter, were always the routine cleaning of brushes and palette plus any mechanical chores like stretching or turning canvases.

All this still left time for other activities, and in Aldeburgh there were plenty on offer. When the Potters first arrived, with *Gamesmanship* still a household word and with Att's show being well reviewed in the national press, they were regarded as an intriguing influx to Aldeburgh society, were called on by well-wishing neighbours and invited to numerous cocktail parties and dinners. Nor were they slow to reciprocate: they enjoyed party-going and entertaining.

With many overlaps, there was a discernible division of the town into golfers, sailors and supporters of the recently started Aldeburgh Festival. Stephen made much use of the golf club and the Potters got to know many from that set. At the same time, however, they were welcomed into the circle of those connected with the Festival. In the very week of our arrival, and before food and bedrooms had been properly sorted out, it was decided that the four of us should eat out at the Wentworth, one of the two main hotels on the front. At the next table were Benjamin Britten, Peter Pears and E. M. Forster. Stephen already knew Britten through BBC work and in 1947 had spent some time with him, John Piper and Eric Crozier preparing and producing a programme about the making of *Albert Herring*. Britten – who liked to be called 'Ben' – had somehow heard of the Potters' arrival in Aldeburgh. He came over, introduced us to his party, welcomed us to the town and offered any help needed over pots or pans or anything else that might have got left behind in the move. An invitation to drinks at his home on the front (Crag House) followed and so began a Crag House/Red House axis that was to develop and to last.

Both Ben and Peter were enthusiastic about my mother's painting. Ben had a similar work pattern. He too disallowed any kind of interruptions in the mornings – and both would usually take the afternoon off. Peter had throughout his life put any spare cash into buying pictures: never as an investment, but in order to have the pleasure of living with a collection that he had chosen. It was not long before he bought his first Mary Potter. In the early days, tennis was often arranged on the public courts. Both Stephen and Att were good players, Peter a hard hitter but slightly erratic, Ben (then not quite forty) considerably better than any of them. However, he had at least found opponents capable of getting the ball back and was glad to play when a four was available. Peter, with a busy programme of recitals, was frequently away; and Stephen was usually in London for some part of the week. But my brother and I were often around to make up the game and Laurens and Ingaret van der Post became regular participants. At The Red House, Stephen soon arranged for the former bowling green to be converted into a grass court, and croquet on a second lawn was also organised. The public courts were forgotten, and tennis afternoons transferred to The Red House.

The Festival, after four seasons, already offered the features that were to make it, for some of its supporters, the world's best. Internationally famous musicians would ask to be allowed to participate, in some cases for nothing. Yet it had a degree of improvisation and informality that gave it an edge over grander festivals elsewhere. At that time, however, it was still only at the turning point as far as support from the town and more general public recognition were concerned, and it is unlikely that its existence played much part in my parents' choice of Aldeburgh as a home. The 1951 Festival was in progress when they were there, just before buying The Red House. Stephen wrote to me in Korea:

> Aldeburgh was mixed up with the annual Benjamin Britten festival, and Andrew and I listened to an hour of Jephtha, an old Handel oratorio exactly like itself all the way through before we escaped from a rather warm church to go off and play golf.

The meeting with Ben and Peter, however, was to open new doors of musical perception and a new circle of friends to the Potters, and by 1954 both of them were on the Festival's Council. The Festival became the highlight of the year and the house filled with guests. Concerts, sessions around our Bechstein getting to know the song cycles, parties, golf and tennis were all fitted in.

Stephen and Att were soon introduced to the other organisers of the Festival. Among those who became lasting friends of my mother was Imogen Holst (Imo), who had arrived in Aldeburgh in the autumn of 1952 to help Ben with the preparation of *Gloriana* and who was to stay on as his musical factotum on matters ranging from copying to research. Att's successful 1954 portrait of Imo still hangs on the stairway of the Maltings at Snape (plate 20). Imo demanded that there should be no interruptions while she was sitting, as she wanted to use the time to go over in her mind the score of Bach's *St John Passion*, which she was to conduct in that year's Festival. (Can this be seen in her expression?) Imo was an unremitting worker, to the point of becoming a recluse towards the end of her life. But she still found time to encourage music among the local non-professionals, and spent many evenings rehearsing The Aldeburgh Music Club.

The Aldeburgh Music Club had been founded by Ben and Peter in April 1952. The large drawing-room in Crag House was used for the gatherings. In February 1953, however, Crag House was made uninhabitable by the North Sea floods. Banks of shingle

Fig. 8 Music Club: JP, Imo, BB, MP

were hurled by the sea across Crag Path into the front garden and piled up against the house. River water rushed down the High Street, swamping the ground floor: for days the basement was a morass of water, coal, coke, rubbish and foul-smelling paraffin. Ben was put up at The Red House for a week. There it occurred to him that the Potters' drawing-room was a suitable venue for the Music Club concert that was to have taken place at Crag House at the end of that week. The offer of the room was elicited and accepted, grateful thanks were recorded in the minutes, and Stephen and Att both joined the Club. Att sang in madrigals and played the recorder. Ben, Peter and Imo regularly participated, but never – in order to preserve the amateur status of the Club – on their own instruments. Thus Ben performed on the viola and treble recorder, while Peter played the piano and bass recorder, and conducted. Concerts were held, usually for members only, for which different groups would have separately rehearsed. The Music Club minutes record that on 21 March 1954 Miss Holst, Mr Britten, Mrs Potter and Julian Potter performed recorder pieces; and fig. 8 shows this quartet in action.

Despite busy musical, sporting and social calendars, Att painted every day, and the gamble of having a housekeeper was working well. Sales were made direct from the studio, particularly during the Festival. Her most sought after paintings were interiors with the Pompeiian

Fig. 9 With Ben at Opera Ball, Festival Hall, October 1952

red background of the drawing-room walls (front cover and plate 21). *The Times* noted that with the use of this colour she had 'broken new ground by varying her predominantly cool tones'.

The year 1953 was a particularly busy one. As well as preparing for her next London show, she entered a three feet by four feet Aldeburgh beach scene (plate 22) for a Contemporary Arts Society prize competition at the Tate on the theme of 'Figures in their Setting'. Probably her largest picture to date, it is about sunlight on open stretches of sky, sea and pebbles: the required figures help with the perspective, but otherwise merge with the beach. In the same year she had three oils in the Graves Art Gallery (Sheffield) exhibition 'Famous British Women Artists'. On top of all this, there was the 1954 Festival calendar. As a contribution to Festival funds, she, John Piper and Prunella Clough had each agreed to prepare four lithographs, so that there would be one for each month. She had not attempted a lithograph for many years and had great difficulty with her first month, but eventually wrote to Kenneth Clark: 'Having got one of them right, I've just got the hang of it now. You can't do anything simply without doing something elaborate first.' She wrote to me: 'I am frantically busy. My show is more or less ready, and packed up to go to London next week. It is making the Aldeburgh calendar that is turning my hair white. I have to be in London all next week making lithographs for it at The Royal College of Art.'

The show referred to in this letter was a watercolour exhibition in June 1953. It was again at the Leicester Galleries, where a second major show of her oils was to be held the following year. The 1954 show was widely reviewed – more so than ever before. Even provincial papers such as *The Newcastle Journal* and *The Yorkshire Observer* wrote about it, because, as was mentioned and commended in *The Scotsman*, Mary Potters were gradually being acquired by public galleries around the country. As with previous shows, the reviewers were respectful and appreciative, without using words calculated to fill the gallery. Thus John Russell in *The Sunday Times*:

> Its first impact is deceptive. So much quietness, so much greyness, so much distilled, refracted light, so subdued and delicate a crust of paint – might all this not make for monotony? It might: but it does not, because Mrs Potter's pictures, so casual seeming, are in fact minutely planned. In the big beach-scapes every fragment of sea-wrack has its place, and keeps it; and the weather is instinct with the fleck and dazzle of the sea.

The indefinable quality of the paintings was touched on by Alexander Lang in *Art News and Review*:

> Mrs Potter's seaside paintings bear the same tenuous relation to the sea itself as do the sounds a child hears when he incredulously obeys his elders' instructions – 'Hold the shell to your ear, dear. Now do you hear the waves?' Likewise, in Mrs Potter's landscapes and interiors, identifiable resonances of time and mood are conveyed delicately and intimately.

Fan letters were, as usual, full of praise. One letter to Stephen from Stephen Spender is worth quoting, simply because it is not addressed to Att:

> … In the best sense, it is feminine. When one looks at these paintings of the sea or a rose one sees that the way women see things really has – through the work of a few outstanding women artists – enriched our sensibility…

Stephen Spender was not the first to describe Mary Potter's art as 'feminine'. Eric Newton said much the same thing (see page 48), which was to be a critical refrain right up to the time when it was no longer socially acceptable to make that point. Att never objected to the epithet, nor would she have dismissed the suggestion that women artists might be able to bring to their work qualities unattainable by men. The trouble was that 'feminine' could so easily be equated in the reader's mind with charm and good taste – and reviewers had to be very careful in their choice of words to avoid that unwelcome connotation.

Att's style at this time was still representational, although she was eliminating more and more detail, leaving only those strokes necessary to convey the essence of her subject. How is it that such a light-handed approach can convey instantly the feeling of the Aldeburgh front in the 1950s (plate 18)? Or how can a few yellow brush strokes seem to say so much about sprigs of forsythia (see cover illustration).

In the autumn of 1952 Att started on the first of many attempts to paint Ben, whom she found a difficult subject. Although he sat still, he was always working, some of the time discussing details of next year's Festival with Imo, who sat out of his sight so that he would not look at her. 'Have had a fearful tussle over a portrait of Ben', she wrote. 'I only have an hour every afternoon doing him at his desk in his writing room. Half the time he is jotting down bits of music. In spite of the fact that he is immensely co-operative, I have made a mess of it. I go to London next week for four days, and when I get back we start all over again!' She struggled with this portrait for five weeks. 'If only you will leave out my face!', was Ben's comment. Peter was not keen on the second attempt either – nor on the much better later portrait of him with his dachshund Clytie sitting on his lap, which Mary later gave to the Britten-Pears library. A good preliminary watercolour for another portrait (not completed) can be seen in plate 26. A portrait of Peter had also been commissioned earlier, in December 1952. It was not hung for long and in his case, no second attempt was made.

Although Stephen's absences in London gave Att more time for painting, all was not well. Their silver wedding was in July 1952. They invited to dinner Ben, Peter and William Plomer, a frequent contributor to Festival events and librettist for *Gloriana*. The talk never flagged, and William's wit kept it light. Ben believed in ghosts, and this fact gave an eerie intensity to his stories of some of the local apparitions. It was a balmy summer evening and it ended with a moonlight game of golf croquet, piano duets played by Stephen and Ben, a sea bathe from Crag House – and slightly fuddled bonhomie. But had the anniversary been a success?

Stephen's diaries show that his emotional life at this time centred around the fact that Heather Jenner, whom he had first met in 1948, was refusing to see him. Day after day the pages are filled with near-suicidal lamentation. Who was seeing her now? How could she be so sadistic? Would he ever see her again? He felt unable to work. Even in the entry describing the silver wedding, two pages are on the dinner party, three-and-a-half on Heather. Att could not have failed to notice the despairing, bitter mood that permeates the 1952 and 1953 diaries, even if she never read them.

Att attempted to cheer him up. After a day or two in town, he would return to the golf, the sunshine, the social life of Aldeburgh and above all to Att, whose company always stimulated him, towards whom he was always affectionate and whom in many ways he never ceased to love. She teased him about his vagueness and tendency to put things off, kept him on his toes with his work and encouraged him in his attempts to get away from the financial shackles of *Gamesmanship* and write on other topics.

In 1954 things changed. Heather began seeing Stephen again and before long her husband announced that he would be naming him as a co-respondent. Stephen had to break this news to Att and records the conversation, commenting: 'P. surpassed herself in her complete and heavenly refusal to make a meal of the situation; was blessedly calm'.

Then Heather indicated that she was not happy with the present arrangement. Rather than fight her husband in the courts, she and Stephen should let him divorce her and get married themselves. This possibility does not seem to have occurred to Stephen until that moment: he asked for twenty-four hours in which to think about it. He dreaded the consequences – losing Att altogether, and having to tell her about it first. But he wanted to live with Heather, and the next day he accepted. He told Att he wanted her to divorce him just as her October show was beginning. He records this too:

> It was awful – awful … She looked rather small, old and shabby as I said it. She turned her head away. Only complaining words: 'such a breach of trust'. But the remark that really stung was 'I'll need a saw to get this off' – of her wedding ring.

Att kept The Red House on for three years after this. At first, little changed, even to the extent that Stephen continued to come down at weekends or for the day, unable to admit to himself that he had forfeited his Aldeburgh life and Att's care and company. But Att was trying to get used to the idea of life without Stephen. These visits were upsetting to her and he was not greeted with the hoped-for warmth. The question of money also obtruded: the regular payments that had been promised were too frequently deferred, and sometimes written off altogether.

Ben and Peter, like many other friends, were shocked at the news and did what they could to soften the blow. The divorce did not come through until May 1955, but in February, not long before Att's fifty-fifth birthday, they persuaded her to come on holiday with them to Zermatt, saying that many people had been known to take up skiing at a much later age than that. Att was still surprisingly athletic, and during the last four years badminton in the Jubilee Hall had often served as a winter substitute for tennis. But the new sport was not a success – her first run down the nursery slopes left her covered in bruises. So while Ben and Peter went skiing, she used the time adapting her style to the Swiss landscapes and came back with about two dozen watercolour sketches. Dramatic grandeur was not her line, but the oils that she worked up from these, seeming to depict smallish, round-topped hills, were unusual and sold well. Another product of that holiday was Ben's *Alpine Suite* for recorders, dedicated to Mary Potter and inscribed '… a tiny memento of a perilous journey, the results of which have made the world so much richer (and I mean *visually!*)'.

Soon after getting back from Switzerland, Ben said that he owed a party to so many friends in town that he would never be able to give one, as his house was not big enough. He suggested that he, Peter and my mother should give a joint party at The Red House, where at least it would be easy to spill over from one room to the next. This was agreed for 12 noon on Easter Monday, invitations were printed and a long guest list drawn up. Practically everyone accepted, and it was realised too late that even in The Red House, it would be impossible to get everyone indoors. The only possibility was to have the party in the garden – and pray for fine weather. It turned out to be one of those hazy blue, windless Easter days that occur once in ten years. The ancient cherry tree was in blossom, the grass had just been cut and the air in the garden was intoxicating even before the party had begun. Several crates of champagne were drunk before the last guest swayed through the gate. Even Imo had a glass or two, and was seen practising her ballet steps while picking up cigarette butts from the lawn.

Six months after this, in October 1955, Ben and Peter embarked on a four-and-a-half-month world tour. The coming winter had for years in advance been kept free of all perform-ing engagements. My mother, left more on her own, began preparing for her 1957 show on the one hand, and supplementing her income with portraits on the other.

In the first three years at Aldeburgh, sitters had been restricted to Ben, Peter, Laurens and Ingaret van der Post, Imogen Holst and Lavinia Russell (daughter of *The Sunday Times* art critic). Since the October 1954 show, Att had been accepting more commissions. One of these was once again for the Nichols family, this time a 'conversation piece' showing Phil and his wife Phyllis with all four children. Another, commissioned by Ben and Peter, was of the Countess of Harewood, the wife of the Festival's president. Att had great difficulty in com-pleting this satisfactorily and it took up much of her time during the first months of Ben's world tour. Twice he wrote urging her to complete it – in November 1955 from Salzburg and in February 1956 from Hong Kong. The end result was however judged a success, was in-cluded in the 1957 show and still hangs in the sitter's home today.

Other pictures were produced with less of a struggle. Att herself thought she was painting well, and expected the show to be a success. Following the Private View, her friends agreed with her. Laurens van der Post wrote: '… I just had a general feeling of a great forward move-ment into the most impressing kind of tranquillity at the heart of your new work'. The reviews on the other hand, while being as favourable in tone as ever, were shorter – even perfunctory. A respectable fifty per cent of the paintings on view were sold, but Att was disappointed, and wrote to Joyce Grenfell: 'I felt sure it was better than other shows I had had, and people whose opinions I value had all been exceptionally enthusiastic. *So* I expected a sell-out!'

The critics did introduce one new element in their comments: for the first time, they spotted an oriental influence. *The Observer* said her work was '… in tune with the Chinese poetry of suggestion'. 'A faintly oriental element' was noted by *The Times* and *The Daily Telegraph* wrote of 'the Japanese subtlety of *Golfers in the Rain*'. Ben and Peter had returned from their world tour full of praise for Balinese music and the spare economy of Japanese Noh plays. The music for *The Prince of the Pagodas* and (later) *Curlew River* had, respectively, been inspired by these enthusiasms. Was it merely coincidence that traces of the Orient in Att's work first appeared at this time?

A Mid-Career Overview

Commentary on Att's painting has been intertwined in this book with the story of her life. Now, with Att approaching sixty, it is time to step back and try and summarise the main features of her work.

The impact of a Mary Potter is not immediate. Her pictures are best appreciated when lived with and looked at over a prolonged period. They repay close observation, particularly of the contrasts of allied but subtly distinct tones and colours. This is especially so of her later, more abstract paintings.

Critics have referred to Mary Potter's restrained and unemphatic palette as 'English'. This leaves open the question of whether our grey and misty climate was responsible for her muted colours, or whether she would have painted in the same way on the Isle of Capri. My view is that she would have found the strong sunlight and colours uncongenial, and would not have stayed there long. Her pictures were not only muted, but matt. The admixture of Parris' Marble Medium took the shine out of the oil paint and the instruction to buyers never to varnish or glaze the paintings made sure that they never shone. They were recessive, and viewers had to find their way into them.

Unobtrusive and quiet, obviously such paintings were not going to 'set the Thames on fire', particularly in comparison with some of her gaudier contemporaries. Her public may well have been small at this time simply because many gallery goers passed her paintings by without noticing them. Yet the slow-burn effect on those who bought her work was remarkable. It is a fact that most of Att's sales at every exhibition were to second- (or third- or fourth-) time buyers. They came back for more because they had found that the longer a Mary Potter hung on their walls, the more they liked it.

Paintings by many other artists looked better in galleries than in private houses, not only because of their larger size, but because they stood out more from a mêlée of different styles on either side. Att's were essentially for the home, in their repose and refusal to shout for attention. They stand the test of being looked at every day. Many letters testify to this.

Another mysterious aspect of the paintings is the way in which they seem to open the eyes of the viewer. Seeing familiar sun, sea and sky effects through the eyes of Mary Potter can make us see them as if for the first time. Or we see a vase of flowers on her canvas more intensely, more fully, than when it is in front of us on the table. Myfanwy Piper, in her introduction to a later catalogue, remarked on this phenomenon:

> It is a fact that we not only enjoy her paintings more and more as our eyes become used to their subtleties, but that through her way of looking at things our own visual sensibility is extended. Like all proper artists she teaches us to see more, and differently.

The same is true of the portraits. It is not just a question of admiring the likeness: we find we have somehow been given a revealing encapsulation of the sitter's character. Even in a pencil sketch, a few deft lines can achieve this.

In his introduction to a later retrospective show, Kenneth Clark wrote: 'What a mistake to bring the heavy engines of analysis and interpretation to bear on Mary Potter's pictures'. Att herself did not theorise about painting, least of all her own. She knew whether a painting had come off or not, and analysis was tedious. Richard Smart felt the same way. He wrote '… the new paintings give me enormous pleasure. Just why I cannot define. Anyway, the better a painting, the less it has to do with words.'

Change of House

During the two years leading up to the 1957 show, Att had come to realise that it would be a mistake to try and keep up The Red House. She could no longer afford to entertain on the same scale and the size of the house emphasised its emptiness. But her search for another was half-hearted. She told herself she was too busy with her show to house-hunt; and the few possibilities she did look at compared so unfavourably with where she was that they were ruled out. Everything about The Red House had suited her: its spaciousness, her studio, and the extensive garden, where throughout the year she could find flowers for the house. But by mid 1957 a move could no longer be postponed. She decided to leave it as soon as the October show was out of the way.

Att becomes Mary

Aldeburgh is over one hundred miles away from London and in those days the journey by car could take as much as four hours. Att kept in touch with her London friends, sometimes going up for the day by train, occasionally staying with them for longer visits. But she ceased to think of herself as a Londoner, immersing herself in her new circle. Neither Ben nor any of her Aldeburgh friends used the Slade name Att: to them she was always Mary; and for the sake of those that survive and may be reading this, she will from now on be referred to by that name. This change may confuse, but it does coincide with a new start to my mother's life and heralds a major change in her painting. Throughout the next ten years she was feeling her way towards a new style and it helped her in this to be slightly dismissive about the whole of her previous output. It may be no coincidence that she now maintained that she had never much liked the sound of 'Att' anyway, and much preferred the name Mary.

1. *John Attenborough* (grandfather) 1921 23 × 19 in.

2. *Evening Sketch* c.1921 9 × 12 in.

3. *Girl with Ukulele* 1922 19 × 15 in.

4. *Lilies and Cigar Box* *c.*1930 19 × 14 in.

5. *Red Mullet* *c.*1928 14 × 17 in.

6. *Swanage Beach* *c.*1936 13 × 15 in.

7. *The Window, Chiswick* 1929 30 × 22 in.

8. *Chrysanthemums c.*1935 24 × 18 in.

9. *Lily of the Valley by the River* 1938 23 × 19 in.

10. *Golden Kipper* 1939 20 × 16 in.

11. *Platt Park* 1940–1 19 × 15 in.

12. *Country Studio* 1944 25 × 33 in.

13. *Rising Moon* 1942 25 × 37 in.

14. *Doves in the Zoo* 1945–6 23 × 19 in.

15. *Peonies* 1947 38 × 29 in.

16. *Early Morning Regent's Park* 1946 21 × 27 in.

17. *Rough Sea, Brighton* (watercolour) *c.*1947 9 × 13 in.

18. *Crag Path, Aldeburgh* *c.*1953 11 × 13 in.

19. *Golfers in the Rain* 1955 19 × 29 in.

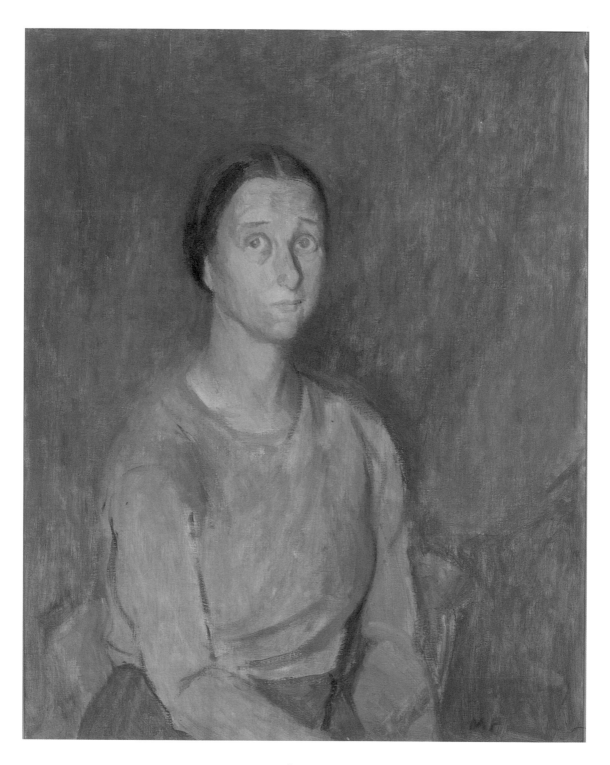

20. *Imogen Holst* 1954 28 × 22 in.

21. *Red Still Life* 1956 24 × 30 in.

22. *Aldeburgh Beach* 1953 36 × 48 in.

23. *East Wind* 1955 24 × 30 in.

24. *St Peter denying Christ* 1958 36 × 30 in.

25. *East Coast Window* 1959 29 × 36 in.

26. *Benjamin Britten* (watercolour) *c.*1960 10 × 9 in.

27. *Rain in Venice* 1961 19 × 23 in.

28. *Still Life with Honesty* 1963 36 × 48 in.

29. Artwork for Festival Programme Cover 1962

30. *A Note from a Cello* (silkscreen print) 1970 18 × 28 in.

31. *Reflected Shapes* 1968 25 × 41 in.

32. *Landscape with Cottages* 1972 45 × 25 in.

33. *Bonfire* 1974 40 × 60 in.

34. *Reflected Patterns* 1974 30 × 36 in.

35. *Studio Wall* 1976 20 × 30 in.

36. *Jar and Leaves* 1977 18 × 31 in.

37. *Rose and Shadows* 1977 22 × 24 in.

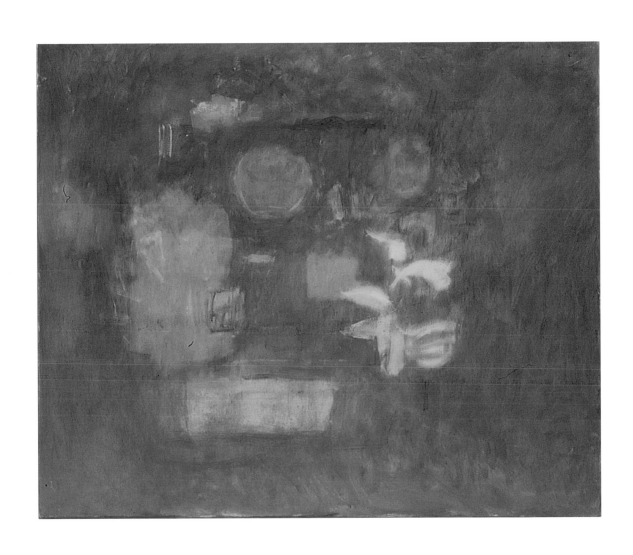

38. *Dark Painting* 1977 35 × 42 in.

39. *Pink Window* 1979 34 × 30 in.

CRAG HOUSE

During Mary's search for a new home, Ben and Peter were also thinking of moving. They wanted something larger, away from the centre of town. They made it clear that when she did move out of The Red House, they would appreciate first refusal; and eventually I asked my mother why the two homes could not be swapped. A swap would cut out much of the financial hassle attached to buying and selling and would be less disruptive for both parties. Tennis could still be played at The Red House, and Crag House could still be used as a base for sea bathing. Crag House had been used by Ben during Festival time as a place where artists performing in the close-by Jubilee Hall could rehearse; and as a place where house guests could have a drink during intervals. From the start it was agreed that both these practices should continue.

Leaving behind the croquet hoops and tennis net, Mary moved into Crag House in November. It is the middle of three joined houses. The front door opens onto the street, with no garden or even pavement. At the east-facing back, there is a small, sunken garden with steps up to Crag Path, Aldeburgh's unpretentious promenade, which runs between the houses and the shingle beach. From the first and second floors, one looked straight out onto the sea: it was almost like being in a boat, with a flag-pole in the shingle as its mast.

Mary's studio overlooked the sea, and the view inspired seascapes in which the wild bleakness of the North Sea contrasts with the placid blue waters of Swanage bay. *East Wind* (plate 23), painted from Crag House while it still belonged to Ben, illustrates the ship effect.

Much the largest room was the drawing-room, which was on a level with the sunken garden. The view in was protected from walkers on Crag Path by a wattle fence and a small, blasted fig tree, which had somehow survived the salty east winds and the onslaught of the shingle in 1953. This was the room used by the Aldeburgh Music Club, and at its meeting there in November 1957, Ben announced that he would be moving. Both The Red House and Crag House were offered for future meetings, but it was not until a year later that the Club again convened at Crag House, with Mary as hostess. A year after that, in September

1959, a new committee was installed, with Mary as chairman, Peter as president and Ben and Imo as vice-presidents. These last three continued to give the Club their unstinting support, with Imo often taking the rehearsals.

Mary still invited a limited number of guests to stay, including the van der Posts, whose own Aldeburgh cottage was closed or let for much of the year. Reciprocal invitations came from her old friend Reine, to one or other of her three homes in London, Wiltshire and Ireland; from Sir Kenneth Clark to Saltwood Castle in Kent, which she visited about twice a year during this period; from the Nicholses to Lawford or from the Meynells to Cobbolds Mill in Monks Eleigh. She nearly always returned from these visits refreshed, having enjoyed the change of scene and company. But at the same time she was beginning to worry that she ought to be spending more time and energy on her work. It was about now that she started to shy away from engagements: a process that was to become more marked later on, and which some may have interpreted as playing 'hard to get'.

No attempt is made in this book to give due weight to or even mention the many friendships that Mary now made as a result of living in the middle of town and being chairman of the Music Club. It may however be relevant to note some of the artists she knew during her thirty years at Aldeburgh. Not that her work was in any obvious way influenced by any of them, but she was intensely interested in what they were painting and some future art historian may be able to trace affinities. She and Prunella Clough, who was then painting brown and grey fishing scenes, were mutual admirers and after their collaboration over the 1954 calendar, Prunella visited Mary a number of times. Philip Sutton, partly on Mary's recommendation, came to live in Snape. He must have been about thirty years younger than Mary. She was excited by his work, although with its extensive use of primary reds and yellows and bright greens it could hardly have been more different from her own. After a few years, Sutton took his family to live in Tahiti, from where he sent Mary cards lavishly illustrated in these gaudy colours. Francis Davison, the collagist, lived in Southwold. His work was not widely known at the time: Mary liked it, and bought a collage made mainly out of brown wrapping paper. At her death, it was the only large non-Mary Potter hanging in her drawing-room. Davison's wife, Margaret Mellis, was also admired by Mary as an artist and they exchanged visits and talked about their work. John and Myfanwy Piper had been friends since pre-Aldeburgh days and now she sometimes went to stay with them in their Oxfordshire home. Through their involvement with the Festival – he as a scene designer, she as a librettist – Mary was now able to see them more frequently. More transiently, Mary often met and got to know the artists who exhibited at the Festival, such as Sidney Nolan. It has been said that Mary Potter worked in isolation. This is true to the extent that she avoided identification with this or that school; but it is certainly not the case that she was unaware of contemporary trends. She would not go to London without fitting in a few exhibitions, and when she became too ill to do that as often as she wanted, in her late seventies, someone would be commissioned to visit selected shows in order to get her the catalogues.

Although pruning back on social activities, Mary did not cut back on her friendship with Ben. Her pocket diaries show that, when he was not away, she would see him two or three times a week. Increasingly, this was without Peter, who at this time was booked up for three years ahead with performances all around the world. Ben on the other hand, whose health had always been less robust – even in childhood there had been something not quite right about his heart – was wanting to spend more and more time in Aldeburgh, composing. He knew East Suffolk so well that he seemed to have in his head every by-road, and he drove Mary on expeditions to remote churches. They walked across the marshes or by the sea. On a few occasions he went sketching with her, and one of his painstaking drawings of Blythburgh church is now in the Britten-Pears Library. Talking about composing music and about painting, they were surprised to find how often they came up against similar problems: for example, how often they both found themselves scrapping what the day before they thought had been an unusually successful morning's work, for the sake of the balance of the complete composition. Like Mary, Ben was distrustful of analysis, believing that music as well as painting should make its impact without the help of literary explanations. A recurring topic was the need to be absolutely firm in keeping enough time each day for creative work, at the expense of other commitments if necessary. Donald Mitchell, the authority on Britten's music, saw both Ben and Mary as 'non-metropolitan', happy to get on with their work in an environment 'untouched by glamour'.

At some point the tradition grew up that Ben and Peter would invite Mary to a turkey and Christmas pudding feast on Christmas night, while she would reciprocate on Boxing Day, usually trying to dish up something as non-Christmassy as possible. The Red House party often included guests from the musical world. On one such Christmas some years on, when my wife and I were also present, I found myself next to Mstislav Rostropovitch, newly arrived from Russia. He had not yet learnt a word of English and talked with Ben and Peter in German. I was placed next to him because of my school certificate credit in that language. Conversation was painfully slow, but became more relaxed after dinner when Ben organised a game of Happy Families. 'Slava, haben Sie bitte der junge Bunge?' my wife found herself saying to the great cellist, speaking German for the first time in her life.

Happy Families became another Christmas night tradition, and Mary produced as a Christmas present a set of Happy Family cards she had painted herself, each one depicting an Aldeburgh acquaintance. Although the names had been changed, each family, and each member of each family, was clearly identifiable. The caricatures were observant and funny, but not cruel. She had taken the trouble to paint the same pattern on the back of every card. The present was a big success and was brought out ceremoniously for a game on subsequent Christmas nights.

For visitors to the Jubilee Hall there could have been few better places to stay than Crag House. Mary had begun taking in lodgers and during the Festival some of these were musicians. Occasionally Festival performers would rush in for a last-minute practice. This was in accordance with the original agreement; but it was more of a Festival bonus than an obligation for Mary and her guests. The idea that Crag House would be used as an interval bar for Ben's guests as well as Mary's was also followed through and this soon became the accepted custom. Cases of drink were provided before the Festival began – I am not sure by whom – and the drawing-room became known as 'Potter's bar'. As well as Red House and Crag House guests, *ad hoc* invitations were extended to members of the audience on their way into the performance. The room would suddenly fill with at least twenty thirsty people, all of whom had to be given a drink and down it within about ten minutes. The two-minute handbell would then be rung in the street outside the Jubilee Hall, extracting concert-goers from the Cross Keys down the road as well as abruptly breaking up the Potter's bar party. Ben's house guests helped to host these occasions: sometimes the Festival's president, Lord Harewood, assumed the role of chief pourer, sometimes this was undertaken by Festival benefactor Prince Ludwig of Hesse, whose widow, Princess Margaret, later became the Festival's President herself, for twelve years until her death early in 1997.

It was the Hesses who were the hosts of Mary's next holiday – at their home at Wolfsgarten, near Frankfurt. In token of thanks, she left behind a small portrait of Prince Ludwig. In 1959 she had her second holiday abroad with Ben and Peter, driving through France and Switzerland to Venice, where for the first time she was able to study the art treasures of that city. Like so many others, she painted the Salute, and also the lagoon looking across to S. Giorgio. The delicate and near-monotone tints in plate 27, showing the base of the Campanile in a rain-swept Piazza San Marco, is typical of her muted reaction to the city. She also did close-ups of the stone-work of palaces, revealing the extraordinary range of soft colours to be seen in a square yard of canal-washed frontage, once bright olive or terracotta.

Again with Ben and Peter, Mary took a holiday in Greece in January 1962. There the rugged scenery and clear light were perhaps incompatible with her soft and misty paintings, although she produced some interesting close-ups of fallen temple stones. The party, which included a couple from the British Council, wanted to see as much as possible in the two-and-a-half weeks allocated and did not settle long enough for Mary to produce more than a few quick sketches in any one place.

Throughout the Crag House years, Mary painted seascapes from her studio window. However inspiring the view, it has to be said that shingle and seawater do not change with the seasons to the same extent as did The Red House garden. I cannot think of one picture painted from this window which is not regarded as a gem by the present owners. But Mary herself was not content to go on indefinitely in the same way. And it was not only a question of subject matter: she was beginning to feel she wanted to go in a new direction. Artists she admired, such as Victor Pasmore,* had for years been painting abstracts. Mary would never have accepted that she was following their lead now; but it may have contributed to her restlessness and desire to experiment.

---

* Pasmore had followed the Potters as tenant of No. 2 Riverside.

A transitory painting was one for another prize competition organised by the Contemporary Art Society, again at the Tate, in 1958. This time it was paintings on a 'Religious Theme'. Mary chose as a subject 'St Peter denying Christ' (plate 24). The painting is more about what is going on in St Peter's mind than a literal representation of any particular scene – although the fig tree and the gate into Crag Path are hovering in the background, alongside a crowing cock. It adumbrates later work in its patchwork effect: the arrangement of colour blocks, dark tones balancing with light, is as important as the objects represented.

East Coast Window (1959, plate 25) was another forward-looking work, more free in its treatment than *East Wind* (plate 23), painted four years earlier. In 1963 it was acquired by the Royal Academy for exhibition at the Tate under the terms of the Chantrey Bequest. The Tate had begun asking artists to write interpretative notes on its acquisitions. Mary still regarded her painting as representational, but her letter to the Tate shows how far she had already shifted from a literal interpretation of that word:

> You couldn't say it was exactly painted from this window … But my studio is right on the sea, and I sort of half paint what I see and half make it up.

Mary's design for the cover of the 1962 Festival programme book (plate 29) went further. Unlike any of the previous covers, the conception was all but abstract, bearing no obvious relation to anything to do with the Festival. The content was spare and she restricted her colours to black and a single shade of blue. 'All but abstract' is accurate, since a close inspection reveals hints of sea birds, pebbles, the sun and a boat: the inspiration is, once again, the view from the Crag House studio window. Mary's paintings always retained a tenuous link with things seen in this way, although latterly even the title of the picture did not make the connection immediately apparent. Sometimes it causes amusement when an apparently abstract painting is given a specific title, such as 'Jug' or 'Wood'. But the title remained important to Mary. It named the object that had set her going, and she regarded it as a clue to a proper appreciation of the picture.

The process was gradual. There was a slow elimination of inessentials; shapes grew hazier. She became more and more concerned with the overall pattern on the canvas and with the balancing of shapes and tones. The title of *Marsh Fire* (1958, back cover) helps to identify the subject matter, but more important is the pattern made by the smoke. Her view of the real world was becoming more and more selective. She grew to dislike the boringness of the horizon line and its divisive effect on the design, and even managed to eliminate it from many of her seascapes. It was a shift from the literal to the poetic.

Mary worked at full stretch while she was at Crag House. While she was living there she had two more shows at the Leicester Galleries, in April 1961 and in March 1963. In June 1961 she also had a large retrospective exhibition at the Minories in Colchester, where no less than forty-seven oils and fifty-eight watercolours were on show. Many of these had been lent by the owners, but a great deal of clerical and other organisational work was involved and a few new works had been painted for the occasion.

The reviews of both London shows were respectful, but the amount of space given to them was small. As with pre-war shows, the usual epithets such as 'feminine', 'modest', 'delicately submissive' and 'sensitive' were again used. Even more than in 1957, however, 'oriental' was now the key word. Her 1963 exhibition was described as 'vaguely orientalised' (*Spectator*); 'an almost oriental deliberation' (Eric Newton in *The Guardian*); 'Chinese sense of delicacy' (Terence Mullaly in *The Daily Telegraph*) and 'oriental simplicity – a few strokes of calligraphic speed and subtle suggestion giving focus to a misty landscape' (Guy Burne in *Arts Review*). Only John Russell in *The Sunday Times* noted the new direction in her work: '… the element of sheer adventure is growing larger, not smaller, with the years'.

Although the six Crag House years were productive and full of activity, they were not her happiest. It was a cold house. I remember Jerry Howard staying the weekend in April 1962, with his wife keeping her fur coat on throughout the Saturday evening. Ben, when he had lived on the sea-front, had been more hardy, taking sea bathes every day before breakfast. Mary was now in her sixties and beginning to feel the chill. During the notorious 1963 cold spell I telephoned to see if all was well. She said that she was able to hold the paint brush in her hand, but only with the help of two oil stoves in the studio, an overcoat and a pair of mittens. Moreover this was also a time for stringent economies. Payments from Stephen were becoming more and more irregular. The Leicester Galleries shows had been successful to the extent that at each one she had sold around half the pictures, but prices then were in two figures only. The Gallery took the normal commission of a third and did not pay for the frames. As a consequence, too much of Mary's time and energy was spent on taking in lodgers.

A smaller house would be cheaper to run, and easier to decorate as Mary chose. Fewer bedrooms would make it impossible to invite so many guests. A new studio would give her a new view, and maybe she would again have one facing north – at Crag House she had been troubled by the alternation of a brilliant, sea-reflected light in the morning and a much-too-dim light for the rest of the day, when the sun soon disappeared behind the steep Aldeburgh houses. Many afternoons were spent looking for a new house; none of those inspected seemed quite right. Then Ben came up with a most welcome proposition. He would build a bungalow-cum-studio in the grounds of The Red House, if Mary would like to move into it 'for a very, *very* reasonable rent'.

CHAPTER 9

RED STUDIO

The Whitechapel

One of the most percipient observers and best explainers in the art world in the 1950s and 1960s was Bryan Robertson, director of the Whitechapel Art Gallery. In an article in *The Times* in January 1964, he argued that Londoners wishing to keep up with the art scene were becoming confused and surfeited. 'They could easily spend every day of each week visiting new shows', he wrote. His prescription was that the public galleries at least should not rush to exhibit every new artist that came along. Instead they should mount in-depth studies of selected artists, showing not just recent paintings, but work over a span of years. Exhibitions should be larger and last longer than the usual West End show and should be backed with educational material. This was the policy he was following at the Whitechapel, and any artist given this treatment was by the same token assumed to be near the peak of his profession. In recent years the accolade of a Whitechapel exhibition had been given, among others, to Jackson Pollock, Sydney Nolan, Henry Moore, Mark Rothko, Barbara Hepworth, Mark Tobey, Anthony Caro and Robert Rauschenberg.

While she was still at Crag House, Bryan Robertson visited Mary and suggested that a major exhibition of her work should be held at the Whitechapel. Normally he chose artists in mid career, whose work was still developing. At first sight, Mary did not seem to fit into this pattern. She was sixty-two, and radical changes seemed improbable – but not to Robertson, who like John Russell had seen the experimental turn Mary's painting had taken. He not only considered her work to be generally underrated, but also believed that new and exciting developments were about to come. He wrote to her in December 1962:

> My own feeling, quite simply, is that you have never had a real chance with your work. You have only been able to exhibit it inside a very restricted and dull framework, and this kind of thing does not present the right kind of opportunity or stimulating challenge to an artist. I believe, absolutely, that your work has an immense potentiality

which is not yet realised. You are eminently capable of realising it and I look forward to the time when your painting really takes off, as they say.

I shall look forward to meeting you in London in January, and working out some kind of date for you. I do not see how we could present the exhibition within less than about eighteen months time (because of existing commitments), but you would need this amount of time to work your way into and to sustain the right vein of painting, on the right scale.

He was suggesting that the show should be both a retrospective and an exhibition of new work. The vast spaces of the Whitechapel walls would never be adequately filled with pictures of the normal Mary Potter size. Bryan Robertson added as a PS some compelling reasons why she should paint on a larger scale:

In good measure you have an original vision; an extraordinarily sensitive feeling for paint or matière in general, and a highly personal and inventive feeling for colour. It would be tragic, with all these gifts, for you to be condemned to producing small cabinet pictures – which are lovely, but are in danger of becoming too easy and thoughtless, I feel. All you need is breathing space and scale and the chance to exhibit the fruits of such an expansion. And now you must have that chance. I've no doubt you will astonish us all.

Mary was elated by this letter. She replied:

If money were no object, I would cancel the Leicester in April, but I think I must press on with that. What a very nice letter you wrote about my painting. I rose onto the top of a near-by cloud! You have given me a lot of confidence, optimism and a great feeling of freedom. I shall indeed need the 18 months …

It was clear that the exhibition was to have a higher proportion of new paintings than was normally the case at the Whitechapel. Richard Smart wrote to her begging her not to forget the outstanding qualities of her earlier work, but in her newfound freedom she wrote again to Bryan Robertson saying, '… this really isn't going to be a *retrospective* at all!'.

Mary would have preferred the show to have been put on in the summer, as she believed her pictures lost out more than those of most artists by not being seen in daylight. However, the Whitechapel was booked until October 1964, and that was the date agreed.

The thought of the physical and creative effort needed to produce so many new large paintings within the time allowed was at first daunting, particularly in view of the limitations of the Crag House studio. Ben's offer to build a bespoke studio in the grounds of The Red House did much to overcome these doubts. She wrote to a friend telling her that Ben 'has enlarged the garden by buying a bit of land adjoining it. He is now building me a sort of studio-bungalow combined. It may be ready in July or August. Thank heaven I shall have a proper *large* studio window and be able to cope with these large pictures.'

Mary moved into Red Studio in September 1963. She had been able to concentrate on her Whitechapel show as soon as she had finished work for the Leicester Galleries show in March; but even before then she had begun to experiment with various ways of adapting to the challenge, four of which can be seen on this and the following pages. The geometric treatment in *Rain* (1962) was followed by the much more conventional *The Cygnet* in 1963. In the same year she painted the mysterious *Window in a Deserted House*, a totally different approach which was to be developed (see *Reflected Shapes*, plate 31). The rounded blocks of

Fig. 10 *Rain* 20 × 24 in.

Fig. 11 *The Cygnet* 30 × 32 in.

colour in *Summer*, on the other hand, were tried in two or three other paintings, but then abandoned. Perhaps more indicative of the direction she was to go in than any of these was *Still Life with Honesty* (1963, plate 28), which shows how much she had benefited from the 'breathing space' she had allowed herself on the canvas. The spaciousness and palely mottled backgrounds, in which colours are painted over each other, are both features of her later work.

Mary had embarked on the most productive period of her life: the Whitechapel show was billed as 'Paintings 1936–1964' but the catalogue shows that of the 115 oils exhibited, no less than thirty-four were dated 1963 or 1964 – and some of these were larger than any she had painted before. Her sea-front studio would not have been big enough: *The Car Park*, a triptych which now hangs in the Britten-Pears School of Musical Studies, measures 48 × 108 in.

Bryan Robertson was delighted with Mary's work and the effect of its display in his gallery. '… The things he said about them were really *glowing*, I would blush to repeat all he said', she wrote. A handsomely produced catalogue had an introduction by Myfanwy Piper and a preface by Kenneth Clark, who also bought *Honesty*. The show was seen by 5,708 people in London and by a further 7,000 odd in Sheffield, where it was hung later in the year. Mary's fan mail was more copious and laudatory than ever before. But when the show was taken down, she felt rather flat. She wrote to Kenneth Clark: 'I didn't expect to have so many come back here again. The ones that have come back are larger than when they left here, because they are framed, so use up my studio space a bit. What with the election hysteria, and Bryan

Fig. 12 *Window in a Deserted House* 30 × 26 in.

Fig. 13 *Summer* 40 × 60 in.

being ill, and what with everyone in Sheffield buying their Christmas presents, the result was disappointing.'

The critics had given the show pride of place in their reviews; but these were not without reservations and many of them could not get over the fact that the Whitechapel, that 'stark cavern of the democratic East End', as one of them put it, the same gallery that had shown Pollock and Rauschenberg, should now be chosen to house Mary Potters. *The Times* began: 'It has taken the most expansive American gestures to fill the Whitechapel Gallery effectively in the past few years. The retrospective of Mary Potter ... must be the most muted occasion the gallery can remember. Certainly the great lights and girders stand out brutally.'

The New Art Centre

The feeling of anti-climax and 'where do I go from here?' was no doubt enhanced by exhaustion following Mary's eighteen-month stretch of work, in the middle of which she had moved house. It was reflected in a feeling that she ought to find a new gallery. It was not just that the Leicester Galleries had moved to Audley Square, which she thought people might have difficulty in finding; it was more that Bryan Robertson had made her realise how much a gallery could do both in promoting her work and in calling forth fresh efforts and new approaches from herself. Kenneth Clark discussed with her the possibilities. He suggested another watercolour exhibition: 'You know how much I love them … I think the best ones equal to the *best* Whistlers'. This idea was not pursued and a question mark continued to hang over the location of the next show. Finally Kenneth Clark put an end to the indecision by suggesting the New Art Centre. He was a founder-patron of this gallery, which had recently been set up by Madeleine Grand and Caryl Whineray. Caryl had previously been assisting Kenneth Clark with the index and notes to his book *The Nude*, and through him, already knew Mary. The change was agreed and a show was booked for May 1967. So began a long and fruitful association. Further shows were to be put on at The New Art Centre in 1969, 1972, 1974, 1976, 1978 and 1980 (not to mention the many exhibitions that Madeleine continued to arrange after Mary's death). Although the intervals between shows were shorter than they had been with Tooth's or the Leicester Galleries, each one consisted of about thirty new oil paintings.

That she was able to go on painting so productively right up to the age of eighty-one was in no small part due to the encouragement and support given her by the gallery, and in particular by Michael Servaes (the son of the manager of the Aldeburgh Festival, Bill Servaes), who joined the New Art Centre soon after it had started. All the NAC directors believed in the quality of Mary's work and had no doubt that her paintings were currently undervalued. They began backing this conviction by buying her paintings themselves, sometimes from auction rooms and sometimes direct from anyone with a Mary Potter to sell. They kept every show open for many weeks and, for each one, their walls were painted with whatever colour Mary suggested. Nothing was too much trouble for them.

Red Studio – Settling In

The other factor behind Mary's continuing productivity was Ben's caring foresight in building Red Studio. The studio itself had an enormous window facing north and ran through to the windowless south-facing garden side. The smallness of the bungalow, after the comparative mansions of Berwick Hall, The Red House and Crag House, must have reminded Mary of her Chiswick Mall days. But it was easy to live in and easy to keep warm. Upkeep was minimal. With her pension and with sales from pictures, therefore, Mary was relieved at last of financial worries.

The opportunity to concentrate on work was seized and Mary began to cut down on other activities. She resigned from her post as chairman of the Aldeburgh Music Club. She had fewer guests to stay. She had always been shy of publicity and disliked giving interviews or writing articles. Now she put an absolute stop on writing or talking about her work for the media. All friends were warned not to telephone her in the mornings and her daily pattern of work extended to Saturdays and Sundays: she could see no reason for wasting two days of the week. During her eighteen years in Red Studio she hardly ever spent more than two or three nights away at any one time. To some, Mary now appeared rather severe and un-approachable; yet she would never have painted the quantity and quality of pictures that she did, without imposing on herself this discipline.

Mary's last journey abroad was in February 1968, when she again went to Venice. Ben had been looking for somewhere to get away from the day-to-day distractions of Aldeburgh, where he could settle down and write *The Prodigal Son*. For this purpose he was staying with Peter in an apartment in the Palazzo Mocenigo, the Venice home of friends of the Hesses. After four weeks in these grandiose surroundings, Peter was due in the United States for a concert engagement, and it had been arranged that Mary should fly out to join Ben for the last fortnight, together with Rosamund Strode, who had succeeded Imo as his musical assistant. This was no holiday. While Ben was writing, Rosamund was correcting proofs and Mary was painting. Work hours were from 8 am until lunch (a picnic), and usually again from about 4 pm until dinner. For Mary it was a productive and successful visit and she returned with a box full of watercolours.

Mary still had time for a few non-painting activities. My wife and I had a cottage ten miles inland, and most weekends we and our three children would see Mary for a meal. My brother Andrew and his two children would occasionally be squeezed into Red Studio to stay, or Mary would put them up in lodgings in the town. Tennis afternoons on The Red House grass court continued. The van der Posts were still among the most frequent guests and Laurens and Mary fought endless battles against Ben and Ingaret. Laurens maintained that The Red House grass court had transformed their summers, from the early 1950s onwards. After tennis, in the cool of Red Studio, she and Laurens would talk about their work. He felt her grasp of art in any field was such that her comments on his own writing were of value. And he was perceptive about her painting, being one of the first to comment on its Chinesey element. He compared her with Chinese artists in her ability to 'go for the essence within the appearances that would conceal it …'. He told of a stormy summer afternoon, when he was racing to get back to town from the marshes before an oncoming cloudburst overtook him. He met Mary hurrying in the opposite direction. 'Can't stop,' she said, 'must see what the puddle near the bend in the river wall looks like in this light.' He later wrote to her from Canada: 'I do so hope that you are well and painting hard the great mysteries with which the puddles, stones, light, earth, trees and other shapes of Aldeburgh are charged and which only you can see and reveal'.

In the late 1960s Ben's deteriorating health often prevented him from joining in his own tennis parties, but he was at home more often. The garden gate at Red Studio led into The Red House garden and it was assumed that he could drop in at the end of the day for a chat, or vice versa, if he or Mary felt the need for company. Yet Ben was at this time still undertaking some performances during the expanding Festival. He remained the keystone of this, planning it and making the major decisions. In this busy schedule, occasionally something would not work out as planned, and it was then, according to Laurens, that the relationship with Mary was of particular value to him. He was inclined to over-react to setbacks, but he would talk the matter through with Mary, who would rationalise and calm the situation down. Laurens said she was to Ben a kind of 'mother confessor'.

Prints and Portraits

In 1969 the Maltings, after only two years' use as a concert hall, was gutted by fire on the first night of the Festival. Ben determined that it should be rebuilt in time for the 1970 Festival. Mary's small but exacting contribution was to prepare a design for a silkscreen print commemorating the disaster, the proceeds of which went towards the rebuilding. It was done in collaboration with William Plomer, whose poem *A Note from a Cello* was integrated into the picture (plate 30). It shows an owl flying across the marshes, with the fire beginning to take hold in the background.

This work was not produced without effort, and involved protracted dealings with the printer, similar to those she had experienced over the jacket design for *Voices from the Crowd*. Intended for the 1970 Festival, it was not available until September. William wrote to her then: 'I can hardly believe that the prints have arrived in Aldeburgh ... my sigh of relief, which I hope is not premature, is strong enough to bend all the reeds flat between Snape and the sea'. Mary was not to produce any more print work.

Mary's last portraits were painted shortly before the 1969 fire. In 1967 Jack Priestley persuaded her to drive over to his house at Stratford-on-Avon to paint his wife, Jacquetta Hawkes. Mary found the concentrated effort of this, on top of the driving, totally exhausting, and when in the following spring she was asked to go back to Stratford-on-Avon to make an alteration to Jacquetta Hawkes's mouth, she said she would take on no further portrait commissions.

There was to be one exception. Later in the same year Joyce Grenfell asked if she could sit, saying she would come to Red Studio for the sessions. Mary agreed. She was fond of Joyce, who alone among my parents' friends had kept up with both of them since the divorce. She wrote a number of letters to Joyce about this project, and some of them are quoted here to give an idea of her approach to portrait work.

I would *love* to paint you – and that time would be very good, as the days will be getting lighter ... The ideal thing is to paint in the mornings, as long as you can bear it. In the afternoon I would like to brood on it and tinker with it ...
31 October 1968

I am rather doubtful about white polo neck or white shirts – it is very difficult to say without seeing them, but white is apt to predominate over the face in a painting. Would pink polo neck go with the sand suit? I can't quite envisage the saffron suit either – if you are coming by car, and it isn't a bother, perhaps better bring the lot and we can sort it out (including the beige jerseys). If we haven't enough colour we can always put it in the background. And thank you for the offer of records, but I *can't* work with music going on, though I know some people can.
22 January 1969

Neither this portrait nor a second attempt, painted in London, was successful. Not giving up, Mary for the first time contemplated the use of a camera.

> I think I shall have to approach this third attempt on the portrait in a different way – from drawings and notes and perhaps a photograph. I *must* get a camera, but if I did I don't suppose I would get good at it all at once. I must get you to advise me. And perhaps if you told me exactly what to do, I could take one with your machine, could I?
> *5 March 1969*

This third version, with Joyce wearing two jerseys and a polo-necked sweater, was kept by Joyce and included in the 1981 Serpentine retrospective.

Deaths and Illnesses

In the late 1960s Mary's mood was buoyant. The first New Art Centre show in 1967 had been a success and only two or three paintings remained unsold when it closed. By the time she left for Venice in 1968 she had four further shows arranged for the next two years. In addition to another at the NAC, there was to be a Mary Potter exhibition at the British Legion Hall at Aldeburgh during the 1969 Festival, and shows at the Oxford Gallery in Oxford, and the Hambledon Gallery in Dorset.

While there was to be hardly any let up in this level of activity for the next twelve years, it was about now that bereavements and the physical pains of old age began in earnest. In 1969 Stephen succumbed to a long and painful illness and died in a nursing home in London. The ties of a long and happy marriage had never been totally unravelled. She wrote to Joyce (who had broadcast a twenty-minute radio tribute the day after he died) a long letter describing the circumstances of his last illness and also the last occasion they had met:

> He managed to get to my private view on November 5th, but he was in a terrible state. Andrew was up for the day and went to fetch him. He came in and collapsed on to a chair. He never looked at the pictures. For one thing, his glasses were so filthy, I wonder he could see anything. I washed them for him and think that was the last thing I had ever been able to do for the poor old boy! … it is all so very, very sad. I would have loved to have had him here, but he has been far too bad for a long time. It is a miracle that he ever got to my show. You are the only one of my friends who understood him – nearly as well as I did.

Meanwhile Ben's health was deteriorating, and as a result he and Mary began to see each other rather less. To get away from the pressure of visitors, telephone calls and the noise of jets from the Bentwaters air base, he and Peter had in 1970 acquired a cottage in deep countryside twenty miles inland, near Horham. There he would often go to work. Although the cottage was a closely guarded secret, Mary was invited to dinner from time to time; but whether Ben was at Horham or not, 'popping round' for a meal, a drink or just a chat became less frequent. He did not have his heart operation until 1973, and did not die until 1976. But for some while before the operation his activities had been severely restricted by his illness. Moreover he knew that he was going to have to undergo major surgery, and was desperately anxious to get the music he had composed down on paper before that happened.

After the operation, Ben's physical deterioration was appalling. Full-time nursing was essential. At the heart hospital, he had come to trust the competence and good sense of one of the nurses, Rita Thomson. He asked her if she would come and live at The Red House and look after him. She did so.

As Mary's contemporaries grew infirm or died, she herself fell prey to a variety of disabilities, including diverticulitis and a bad knee. She gave up tennis altogether at the age of seventy and soon afterwards bought a wheelchair so that she could paint from that whenever necessary.

Mary's seventy-fifth birthday was one of the few happy occasions of those years. Ben had always held that far more fuss should be made of the seventy-fifth birthday – the three-quarters of a century mark – than any other. Seventy was too young to celebrate, eighty was too old and often too late. He gave a party for a few of Mary's friends and family (including five grandchildren) using what used to be the Potter ping-pong room and junk-attracting outhouses of The Red House, but which had now been transformed into the Britten-Pears Library. He rallied himself sufficiently to propose a toast to Mary from his wheelchair.

Just over a month before Ben's death in 1976 Mary wrote to Kenneth Clark: 'Ben is back again, but I am rather glad you didn't see him – as it would have depressed you. When I say I had lunch with him – what it is, is that I go in and have a drink – he *always* says "Forgive me not getting up, dear" – then the nurse hauls him out of his chair – we go slowly to the dining-room – have something rather slight – he can't talk when he is eating, only a few words, so the nurse and I chatter, and then he goes to bed. He is surrounded by people who would do anything in the world to help him, so it is all quite cheerful, but a shock to people who haven't seen him for some time.'

Kenneth Clark

The person closest to Mary after Ben's death was Kenneth Clark – by now Lord Clark. Known as 'K' to his own circle, his formidable reputation as an art historian and appraiser had recently spread to a wider public through his television series 'Civilisation'. Mary had known him since the war, when he had been director of the National Gallery. Her respect and affection for 'K' was to grow over the years and meant much to her. Yet she always kept her friendship with him to herself, in a separate compartment of her life.

At Harley Street, the Potters and the Clarks occasionally went to each other's dinner parties; but by 1949, when Stephen was so often busy elsewhere, Mary and K would some-times lunch together, or perhaps dine out. He had been brought up in East Suffolk and had developed a habit of going back there whenever he needed to write. He describes in the second volume of his autobiography, *The Other Half*, how ever since childhood Aldeburgh had had the effect of sharpening his mind. He mostly stayed at the Wentworth Hotel and in May and June 1952 had booked a room there solidly for some weeks to work on his current book, *The Nude*. Thus Mary's move to Suffolk the previous year did not end these occasional meetings: she saw him in Aldeburgh and she would still lunch with him on her trips to London – or accept invitations to Saltwood Castle.

During the 1957 Festival K was scheduled to lecture on Samuel Palmer, and instead of staying at the Wentworth as usual, he stayed at The Red House. K found the peaceful atmosphere of Mary's home even more conducive to good writing than the hotel. He was to come a number of times to Crag House, and by the 1970s, was one of the few guests she had to stay at Red Studio. Although past retiring age, Kenneth Clark was still writing books, giving lectures and sitting on committees. Visits to Mary seem to have provided him with an opportunity to recuperate from all this and to write, free from distraction. In the evening, he would read over to Mary what he had written, asking for comments. He wrote of her in his 1974 autobiography:

> Her husband, the noted humourist, left her. Of all the women in the world whom I would not have left, Mary Potter is the first. She accepted the law of nature, and went on painting better than ever ... Whenever I have been ill (which, thank God, is very seldom) I have stayed with her to convalesce, and in her peaceful companionship have regained my health.

Kenneth Clark also writes in *The Other Half* of how much he valued the friendship of women, whom he found to be more sympathetic as companions than men. Mary had fulfilled this role since 1949, but there was a short period in the late 1970s when their relationship changed gear and they were in touch by letter or telephone every day. K was now a widower and Mrs Secrest, his biographer, suggested in her book that marriage was discussed. It was indeed, but was never for a moment a practical proposition. He would not have wanted to live in Aldeburgh any more than she would have wanted to leave Red Studio.

Development of Painting

Mary's renown grew as the NAC had predicted. The Tate Gallery bought a third Mary Potter (*Bonfire*, plate 33) and the Arts Council bought a fourth. In her painting, Mary's paring down of the real world went even further. Balance of shapes and colours was what mattered. In a *Sunday Times* review of the 1978 NAC show, Marina Vaizey described the tenuous link with objects that the paintings still had:

> She sometimes calls them 'make-ups'; she draws a lot, from reality, and from these real shapes orchestrates tender still lifes of the imagination. Pale shapes loom in the rich

half-darkness. The imagination arranges and rearranges reality, not the reality of extremes, but of daily life. Buildings are half glimpsed in rain, leaves are stuck into a jar, flowers gleam in the half light. These paintings are hinged on reality and experience, but Mary Potter's allusive, sensitive imagination leaves room for ours.

Mary herself describes the same link in her reply to a letter from the Tate asking for elucidation of *Bonfire*:

> ... It is certainly not meant to be *representational*. I haven't been *that* for a great many years. I don't suppose it is abstract – I don't know what I call myself – I just go on following my inclinations. Outside my studio window I have a mass of tall pine trees, growing close together, and they make marvellous shapes against the sky....The thing that started up this one the Tate has got was that sometimes a gardener will make a bonfire among the trees – As the smoke goes in clouds through the trees, they are crossed with paler, transparent passages, which is very beautiful. I don't think I made this obvious when I got going with the usual business of balancing the colours and shapes. The tiny figure is the gardener! There are no intermediate sketches or anything, or any other versions – I just built it up as I went along. (I did it rather quickly, though some small pictures take months.)

The bits and pieces that triggered an idea for a painting were often unexpected, if not bizarre, details – such as a twig floating in a pool or the surface of faded brickwork. Mary often mentioned her liking for the paintings of Frances Hodgkins, who worked in much the same way. Hodgkins wrote in a 1929 letter from France: '... I have not lifted up my eyes higher than the red earth or the broken earthenware strewn about and making such lovely shapes in the pure clear light ...'.* Caryl Whineray (who by now had married artist John Hubbard) wrote to me about this aspect of my mother's work soon after she died:

> It was also very revealing to me to see her selective eye at work; how she would often pass over what one might have designated in advance a 'Mary' subject. In particular I remember a painting she did of a dilapidated box of broken grey soldiers!

A notable exhibit of the 1978 show was a three-panelled wooden screen, each panel two feet wide and six feet high, painted on both sides. It had been commissioned for the Britten-Pears library. The three panels on one side were called 'Day', in a range of pinks drifting around a sun on the centre panel; the other side, 'Night', in mauves and purples with a lamp discernible in one corner. It was a remarkable feat of energy to cover seventy-two square feet of board, standing on a shoe box to reach the top (Mary was short, and in her late seventies). The screen is now in the Manchester City Art Gallery.

---

* Letter quoted in *Modern English Painters* by John Rothenstein.

At an age when the work of some artists becomes comparatively predictable, Mary's continued to evolve with each show. Laurens van der Post wrote of one of her later shows:

> I was very excited by it because, as always with your work, I felt that you had moved far on your own particular road. There was nothing repetitive or taken for granted about it all. It is lovely the way you always search ahead of yourself …

Kenneth Clark also made the point: 'Each new batch is a surprise'.

The hundreds of paintings that Mary produced in her Red Studio years and the gradual evolution of her ideas deserve a comprehensive study such as is outside the scope of this book. Meanwhile some idea of the development of her later work and its wide imaginative range can be seen in plates 31–39, which are in chronological order and range from 1968 to 1979.

Against the Odds

In 1979 Mary's health became a much more serious problem. Tests for a succession of un-explained pains were inconclusive, but the cause was probably the beginning of the lung cancer that eventually killed her in 1981. She had always smoked an average of forty cigarettes a day, and violent and embarrassingly long fits of coughing now precluded any visits to concerts. Her friends were now nearly all much younger than she was, and she was helped in her illness by constant visits. Tim Fargher, a young artist from Orford, would come over and discuss painting with her and often take her back for a meal with his wife Lizzie, sister of Michael Servaes. Julia Allen, niece of Mary Allen, had a flat in Aldeburgh, loved Mary and was increasingly helpful as her symptoms got worse.

These and other friends helped Mary to keep working. Tim Fargher remembers how she held that artists should never let any real or imagined difficulties stop them from pressing ahead with the application of paint to canvas. To an old family friend who was starting to paint she wrote:

> *Draw* all the time, anything and everything, and you will find things begin to happen. The only answer is to keep on doing it – particularly when you are *not* in the mood, and your potentialities will develop.

In writing this, Mary was of course recommending the same sort of discipline as she applied to herself. She faltered at the age of eighty. At her birthday party, she complained to her artist friend Margaret Mellis that she was going through a dud patch, and was stuck. Margaret Mellis wrote and told her:

> What is so extraordinary is that you haven't ever stuck before. Bill Coldstream stuck for several years and almost everyone I know stuck for months on end. Ben Nicholson once said 'you always think you'll never paint again, but you always do', which I remember when work gets difficult with quite a lot of comfort!

This encouragement helped, and in due course a few more Mary Potters were produced, all painted from her wheelchair.

Some thought that the 1978 show had been her last, and this impression was reinforced by the award of an OBE in 1979, as if to crown her career. But further shows were arranged at the NAC and in Aldeburgh for 1980. Moreover, in the same year the director of the Tate Gallery, Alan Bowness, set aside a room at the Tate for an exhibition in honour of Mary Potter at the age of eighty. As well as the Tate's own three pictures, seven paintings were displayed, including the screen. A party was arranged to launch the show and Mary sat through it, entirely happy, both with the honour done her by the Tate and with the chance to see again her old friends, who included Richard Smart, Kenneth Clark and the Pipers.

Serpentine

Again many thought that the 1980 NAC and Tate exhibitions would be Mary's swansong and that with her illness, she could now honourably retire. But a still more ambitious project was already well under way. Dr David Brown of the Tate considered that another large Mary Potter retrospective was overdue, and since 1979 had been planning this jointly with the NAC and the Arts Council. The proposal was that it should be held at the Serpentine Gallery in Kensington Gardens. This gallery, formerly an old tea house between the bridge over the Serpentine and the Albert Memorial, had recently been acquired by the Arts Council, which had adopted a policy of exhibiting alternately the work of new painters and major retrospectives of established painters. I had earlier taken Mary there to see a John Hoyland exhibition, and she had been impressed with the daylight-filled gallery and its splendid views out to the Gardens and Hyde Park. It was large enough to hang a full-scale retrospective, while at the same time lacking the weightiness of the Tate and with none of the austerity of the Whitechapel, in comparison with which its architecture was almost domestic. It was the perfect showcase for her paintings, and Mary could not but be pleased with the idea. But at first only two rooms of the Serpentine's four had been offered and, on the advice of the NAC, she held out for the whole gallery. She had after all filled the Whitechapel in 1964, and now had twice as many pictures to choose from. She wrote to Sue Grayson, who was handling the project for the Arts Council:

> I feel sorry about the Serpentine as it is such a lovely gallery and it would be nice to be under your auspices – I think the point is that if it would be shared by other artists in other rooms it would be like having another show. As I am having one at the New Art Centre in May and followed by the Festival show in June – it might be better to wait a bit longer for a more isolated retrospective – wish I were a bit younger!

Eventually the Arts Council agreed not only to give over the whole gallery to the retrospective, but also to defer it to the late spring of 1981, so as to be able to display the paintings by daylight alone.

David Brown now took on the task of seeing as many Mary Potters as possible around the country, shortlisting the best for inclusion in the show and persuading the collectors to lend them. Mary had the final say in the selection and did not always approve of David Brown's liking for her earlier work. She wrote to Sue Grayson:

> The trouble with David Brown is that he likes everything! He went to supper last week with my younger son Julian where there was one quite early painting which I thought might be useful – But he liked the lot!

Later she must have relented, as many of her best earlier works were shown.

The date was set for the end of May, but Mary was becoming increasingly worried that she might not survive that long. Those who were organising the exhibition – Madeleine (by this time Madeleine Ponsonby), Michael Servaes, David Brown and Sue Grayson – felt they could only consult her on a very few key issues, as they knew how ill she was. With this in mind, Sue Grayson wrote to say that she need not worry at all about the hanging, as she (Sue) and Michael could easily handle it. But hanging had always been of crucial importance to Mary. Fearful that she would never get to the Serpentine, she sent a letter of guidance to Sue in March, which included the following general instructions:

> One thing is, never to hang two pale light-in-tone paintings together. People say – Oh those two go together, but they do *not* – they make each other look wishy washy. At the same time two dark ones are hopeless together – they make each other look dirty and murky. But put the light and the dark side by side, and everything that is meant in the paintings comes to light.
>
> Another thing – if there is anything predominantly red, it looks awful against anything predominantly blue. I don't know why, but there it is.

Rita Thomson, who had nursed Ben and stayed on at The Red House after his death in 1976, was now coming into Red Studio two or three times a day to care for Mary – despite the fact that she was also nursing Peter, who had himself had a severe stroke at the beginning of the year. She and Dr Ian Tait were determined to do everything possible to control the course of Mary's illness sufficiently to enable her to be present at the show. Mary herself had also been fighting to achieve this. When the time came, she not only got up to London – driven by friends and accompanied by Rita – but even put in an appearance on the afternoon before the private view to check (and marginally change around) the hanging.

On the day itself the chestnut trees were at their peak, the rolling grass of the park had just been cut and the sun shone. No artificial light in the gallery was allowed or needed. Ninety-eight oils were on show, together with many watercolours. The paintings represented the very best of her work from every period. Mary had never written about her life, but the exhibition was itself an autobiography, each painting recalling the house or area she had been living in at the time. Many of Mary's friends had become, like herself, infirm, but most managed somehow to get to the private view – including Peter Pears, with the help of a stick.

For the first time it was possible to see the full range of Mary's achievement and for visitors and critics alike, there was no doubt that this was a magnificent show. Mary presided from her wheelchair all day, re-examining old paintings and renewing old friendships. Although she always professed to dislike private views, on the grounds that they were so exhausting, and although this one no doubt exhausted her more than any, she must have derived great satisfaction from the occasion, the setting, the skill with which the paintings had been selected and hung, and, afterwards, from the unstinting praise she received, both in the national press and on such programmes as 'Kaleidoscope' and 'Critics' Forum'. For once there were no reservations. Almost 25,000 people visited the exhibition. Just as the Whitechapel show had begun her eighteen years at Red Studio with a flourish, so did the Serpentine retrospective round them off. No better finale could have been devised.

Epilogue

As expected, once Mary got back to Red Studio the lung cancer quite rapidly got worse. Its course was eased by constant visits from Rita and her well-liked and trusted doctor, Ian Tait. She still made efforts to work. The retrospective, after over a month at the Serpentine, moved on around the country to King's Lynn, Sheffield and Chichester, and was not dismantled until 10 October. During this time, letters of appreciation continued to come, many of which Mary was able to answer.

Mary's interest in painting did not diminish. Lying in bed, exhausted on her return from the Serpentine, she insisted on watching a television programme on Bridget Riley: she watched to the end, although disoriented by the brightly coloured parallel lines on the screen. She even painted. No longer able to move into the studio, on Tim Fargher's suggestion she experimented with gouaches, sitting in an armchair. Rosamond Lehmann, who had a house ten miles away in Yoxford, visited her a number of times in the last month or two, and her last works were blurred but clearly recognisable sketches of Rosamond. Thus, clear headed and working until very nearly the end of her life, Mary died at home on 14 September 1981.

The Tate made a special display of *Bonfire*, with a bowl of flowers in front of it and a plaque below with the inscription 'Mary Potter: 1900–1981'.

APPENDIX I

ONE-MAN EXHIBITIONS

1932 Bloomsbury Gallery

1934 Redfern (with Edna Clarke Hall)

1939 Tooth's

1946 Tooth's

1949 Redfern (watercolours)

1951 Leicester Galleries

1953 Leicester Galleries (watercolours)

1954 Leicester Galleries

1957 Leicester Galleries

1961 Leicester Galleries
The Minories, Colchester (retrospective)

1963 Leicester Galleries

1964 Whitechapel (retrospective)
Also shown at Graves Art Gallery, Sheffield

1967 New Art Centre
Fermoy Art Gallery, King's Lynn

1968 Oxford Gallery, Oxford

1969 Aldeburgh Festival
New Art Centre

1970 Hambledon Gallery, Blandford Forum

1972 New Art Centre

1974 New Art Centre

1976 Aldeburgh Festival
New Art Centre

1978 New Art Centre

1980 Tate Gallery
New Art Centre
Aldeburgh Festival

1981 Serpentine, London
This retrospective was also shown at:
Fermoy Art Gallery, King's Lynn
Mappin Art Gallery, Sheffield
Pallant House Gallery, Chichester

SELECTED MIXED EXHIBITIONS

1920   New English Art Club
(and subsequently)

1922   Seven and Five Society
(and subsequently)

1927   The London Group
(and subsequently)

1936   Tooth's

1939   Leicester Galleries (little pictures exhibition)

1940   *15 Women Painters*, Leicester Galleries
Tooth's

1949   Recent purchases by the Contemporary Art Society (CAS)

1950   *The Private Collector* – CAS at Tate

1951   Arts Council Festival of Britain Exhibition: *50 Artists: British Painting 1925–1950*,
New Burlington Galleries and at Manchester City Art Gallery

1952   *Seventeen Collectors* – CAS at Tate

1953   *Famous British Women Artists*, Graves Art Gallery, Sheffield
Figures in their Setting – CAS at Tate

1956   *The Seasons* – CAS at Tate

1958   *The Religious Theme* – CAS at Tate

1966   *Painters in East Anglia* – Arts Council travelling exhibition

1967   Royal Scottish Academy: Scottish Society of Women Artists

1975   *Artists of East Anglia*, Radlett Gallery, Herts.

1977   *Real Life* – John Moores Liverpool Exhibition 4 at Walker Art Gallery

1980   John Moores Liverpool Exhibition 12 at Walker Art Gallery (prizewinner)

POSTHUMOUS

The New Art Centre continued to hold Mary Potter exhibitions until that gallery moved from London at the beginning of 1994.

From 1989 to 1990 a touring retrospective was organised by the Oriel 31 Gallery, Newtown and was shown there and in Welshpool and in Kendal, Bath, Norwich and Lincoln.

The Fine Art Society in Bond Street put on a watercolour exhibition in April 1996.

A Mary Potter exhibition extended to two galleries in Aldeburgh during the 1991 Festival and a retrospective of her life's work is planned there for the 1998 Festival. This will move on to The Fine Art Society, London in July and to the Brighton Museum and Art Gallery for two months at the beginning of 1999.

APPENDIX II

PAINTINGS IN PUBLIC GALLERIES

AUSTRALIA

Adelaide

*Highgate House** 1938 – Art Gallery of South Australia (acquired 1948)

Red Still Life 1956 – Art Gallery of South Australia (acquired 1957)

The Thames at Chiswick (lithograph, 1938) – Art Gallery of South Australia (acquired 1941)

Melbourne

Peonies 1947 – National Gallery of Victoria (acquired 1948)

Toys 1977 – National Gallery of Victoria

Sydney

Jessamine 1943 – Art Gallery of New South Wales

Honeysuckle on Wall – Desborough Gallery

CANADA

Montreal

*Still Life with Roses** 1954 – Montreal Museum of Fine Arts (acquired 1956)

Ottawa

Early Morning, Swanage 1948 – National Gallery of Canada (Massey Collection, acquired 1948)

NEW ZEALAND

Wellington

The Studio 1966 – National Museum of Wellington (acquired 1967)

UK

Aberdeen

Carnations 1949 – Aberdeen Art Gallery

Cambridge

Two watercolours – Fitzwilliam Museum

Charleston

Swanage watercolour *c.*1936 – (acquired *c.*1953)

Harrogate

*Deserted Pier** 1948 – The Mercer Art Gallery (acquired 1956)

Huddersfield

The Shed 1966 – Huddersfield Public Art Gallery (acquired 1967)

Hull

Rising Moon 1942 – Ferens Art Gallery (acquired 1946)

Kirklees

*Reflected Patterns** 1974 – Kirklees Collection (acquired 1979)

Leicester

Hellebore – Leicester Education Authority (acquired 1954)

London

Golden Kipper 1939 – Tate Gallery (acquired 1940)

East Coast Window 1959 – Tate Gallery (acquired 1963)

Bonfire 1974 – Tate Gallery (acquired 1974)

Still Life 1959 – Tate Gallery (acquired 1988)

The Window, Chiswick 1929 – Tate Gallery (acquired 1990)

Sgt. Anita Flateau 1942 – Imperial War Museum

Manchester

Night and Day (3-panelled screen, 1978) – Manchester City Art Galleries

Hampshire Farm 1939 – Manchester City Art Galleries

Still Life 1941 – Manchester City Art Galleries

The Thames at Chiswick (lithograph, 1938) – Manchester City Art Galleries

Merthyr Tydfil

*Still Life** 1946 – Cyfartha Castle Museum (acquired 1949)

Norwich

The Mere 1958 – Castle Museum (lent in 1962 by Norfolk Contemporary Art Society)

Sheffield

End of Daylight 1954 – Graves Art Gallery (acquired 1965)

Still Life with Vase 1967 – Graves Art Gallery (acquired 1978)

Evening Light on Trees 1971 – Graves Art Gallery

The Corridor 1970 – Graves Art Gallery

*Winter Landscape, Essex c.*1944 – Graves Art Gallery (acquired 1969)

Southampton

Frieze 1978 – Southampton Art Gallery

*Setting Sun c.*1953 – Southampton Art Gallery (donated 1988)

Grasses and Shadows 2 1973 – Southampton Art Gallery (donated)

Swindon

Burning the Leaves – Swindon Museum (bought in 1956 from the Tate exhibition)

* Bought and presented by the Contemporary Art Society

PAINTINGS IN PUBLIC COLLECTIONS

Arts Council

Regents Park 1949 – purchased 1950

The Erica House, Kew 1951 – purchased 1951

Sun on Beach 1961 – purchased 1961

Dark Painting 1977 – purchased 1978

Government Art Collection

*Blue Jar c.*1945 – purchased 1948

*The Marsh c.*1956 – purchased 1958

*A Girl Skipping c.*1954 – purchased 1964

Birds 1962 – purchased 1964

The Evening Window 1970 – purchased 1972

Trees reflected in Glass 1972 – purchased 1973

Fig. 14 Mary in old age, photograph by Nigel Luckhurst

LIST OF PLATES

COLOUR PLATES
Oil paintings except where otherwise specified

BLACK AND WHITE FIGURES

INDEX

Published by

Scolar Press · Gower House · Croft Road · Aldershot · Hants · GU11 3HR · England
Ashgate Publishing Company · Old Post Road · Brookfield · Vermont · 05036-9704 · USA

First published 1998

British Library Cataloguing in Publication Data
Potter, Julian
Mary Potter
1. Potter, Mary, 1900-1981 - Criticism and interpretation
2. Painting, English 3. Painting, Modern - 20th century - England
I. Title
759.2

LIbrary of Congress Catalog Card Number 98 - 071509

Hardback ISBN 1 84014 208 1
Paperback ISBN 1 84014 640 0

Produced for the publishers by John Taylor Book Ventures
Faringdon, Oxfordshire
Designed and typeset in Garamond by Lovelock & Co and printed in Great Britain
at the University Press, Cambridge

MARY POTTER

A LIFE OF PAINTING

Julian Potter

SCOLAR PRESS

MARY POTTER

A LIFE OF PAINTING